# IF IT WEREN'T
## FOR THE
# LOVE OF GOD

# IF IT WEREN'T FOR THE LOVE OF GOD

**ALEXYS V WOLF**

If It Weren't for the Love of God

Copyright © 2025 by Alexys V. Wolf. All rights reserved.

No part of this publication may be reproduced, stored in a retrieval system or transmitted in any way by any means, electronic, mechanical, photocopy, recording or otherwise without the prior permission of the author except as provided by USA copyright law.

Scripture quotations marked "NAS" are taken from the New American Standard Bible®, Copyright © 1960, 1962, 1963, 1968, 1971, 1972, 1973, 1975, 1977, 1995 by The Lockman Foundation. Used by permission. All rights reserved.

Cover design by Ira of FIVERR
Interior design by Pooja of FIVERR
Editor Pamela Scholtes

The opinions expressed by the author are those of The Fiery Sword Global Ministries.

---

The Fiery Sword Publications
Lexington, SC

Published in the United States of America

ISBN: 978-1-952668-73-9

1. Books › Religion & Spirituality › Christian Books & Bibles › Ministry & Evangelism › Evangelism
2. Books › Religion & Spirituality › Christian Books & Bibles › Christian Living › Inspirational
3. Books › Religion & Spirituality › Worship & Devotion › Faith

# Table of Contents

Dedication ............................................................vii
Foreword................................................................ix
Introduction.......................................................... 1

Chapter One: God is Love ..................................... 3
Chapter Two: What His Love Accomplished for Mankind ......................................... 15
Chapter Three: The Wedge Between Us and God's Love.................................... 21
Chapter Four: My Selfless Praying Father ............. 27
Chapter Five: Experiencing God's Love ................ 37
Chapter Six: Eternal Life and Love ....................... 45
Chapter Seven: I Am Nothing Without Love ....... 53
Chapter Eight: God's Loving Discipline ............... 61
Chapter Nine: How Does God See Love?............. 67
Chapter Ten: Love Your Enemy as Your Neighbor ......................................... 75
Chapter Eleven: God's Perfected Love .................. 83

## TABLE OF CONTENTS

Chapter Twelve: What About the Fatherless? ........ 93
Chapter Thirteen: A Forgiving God .................... 103
Chapter Fourteen: Freedom for Freedom's Sake ... 109
Chapter Fifteen: Story of My Failure and
                        Redemption ............................ 115
Chapter Sixteen: Nonconformist ........................ 123
Chapter Seventeen: How to Bask in God's Love .... 131

Closing Prayer .................................................... 139
Introduction to Christ ......................................... 141
Author's Catalog ................................................. 153
Author Bio ......................................................... 155

## Dedication

To my daddy, Retired Lexington SC Police Chief Mike Roth, the greatest expression of God's love from father to child I have witnessed.

# Foreword

<u>If It Weren't For the Love of God</u> is a book that speaks straight to the heart—especially for those new to faith or who feel like they've drifted too far from God to find their way back.

It's not full of religious jargon or complicated theology. Instead, it's honest, transparent, and deeply personal. Author Alexys V. Wolf shares real struggles—moments of doubt, failure, and feeling lost—but always brings it back to one powerful truth: God's love never gives up on us.

Whether you're just beginning your walk with Christ or trying to find your way home again, this book reminds you that you don't have to have it all together. God's love is not earned—it's given. Freely. Patiently. Unconditionally.

<u>If It Weren't For the Love of God</u> is like a beacon of light in the darkness for anyone who wonders if God still cares. The answer in these pages is a resounding "*Yes!*" If it weren't for the love of God, none of us would make it—but because of His love, there's always a way forward.

# FOREWORD

My favorite quote is in chapter eight, where she says, *"Sin separates us from His blessings and presence, which is different from being separated from His love."* That clarifies a lot! I, as well as many I know, have wondered if one of my sins was just too much for God to forgive and if He would still love me after doing such a thing. So, this stood out to me personally.

This book is perfect for those who need a fresh start or a gentle reminder of who God is!

Author Helen T. Melcher

# Introduction

> "…being rooted and grounded in love, may be able to comprehend with all the saints what is the width and length and height and depth, and to know the love of Christ which surpasses knowledge, that you may be filled to all the fullness of God (Ephesians 3:17-19)."

In early 2025, my eldest daughter, Sophia, asked if I had a book specifically geared toward God's love. Since I did not, I decided to pen this book for her and anyone seeking to understand God's love and how He generates such love within mankind.

Sadly, there is too little understanding concerning His love within Christ's body, not because He didn't make it available but because we haven't properly sought Him. Yes, we say, "*God loves me/him/her/them,*" yet with little to no genuine comprehension of His love's depth and power. This is why so many of God's people are stuck in the doldrums of life, frustrated, sad, depressed, angry, irritated, conflicted, hopeless, lifeless, and more of the like. This should not be.

## INTRODUCTION

Granted, we all feel myriad emotions on any given day, but those emotions should not be our way of life. Emotions wax and wane, but God's eternal love is steadfast and ever-present. Because of this fact, we should be readily able to pull ourselves out of our emotions, confident in who God is, His unwavering love for mankind, and who we are in Him.

Within these pages, we will explore the depth of God's love for mankind and how He loves us from various roles. Much of this book is taken from other books I have written about His love. I simply pulled previous writings and added fresh insight. I am a "*If it ain't broke, don't fix it*" gal!

**CHAPTER ONE**

# God is Love

Beloved, let us love one another, for love is from God, and whoever loves has been born of God and knows God. Anyone who does not love does not know God, because God is love. By this, the love of God was revealed in us, that God has sent His only Son into the world so that we may live through Him. In this is love, not that we loved God, but that He loved us and sent His Son to be the propitiation [appeasement or atoning sacrifice] for our sins. Beloved, if God so loved us, we also ought to love one another. No one has ever seen God; if we love one another, God remains in us, and His love is perfected in us. By this we know that we remain in Him and He is us, because He has given to us of His Spirit. We have seen and testify that the Father has sent the Son to be the Savior of the world (I John 4:7-14).

To kick off this book, we must first know that God is love. He cannot be anything short of love, which is from everlasting to everlasting. Psalm 103:17 (NIV) reads, *"But from everlasting to everlasting, the Lord's love is with those who fear Him, and His righteousness with their children's children."* Other versions replace "*love*" with "*mercy.*" Mercy is God's eternal love upon undeserving mankind.

Because He is love, He sent His only Son, the firstborn of Heaven, to live in a fallen world, in a sin-stained, earthen vessel, to be rejected by His creation, mocked, spit on, reviled, slandered, wounded, and crucified for us. What human do you know who would do that for those they love much less their enemies? Sure, we all want to believe we would, but most have not had to face even a fraction of such a situation.

We are redeemed from sin, death, and Hell through God's merciful love. He loved us completely before He breathed life into Adam's nostrils. He knew Adam would sin and that He would have to sacrifice His Son to bring us back to Him.

I don't believe anyone can fully comprehend God's love this side of Heaven, but I dive into it headfirst, intending to bask in it as much as He will allow! He loves us so completely that Ephesians 3:17-21 says, *"so that Christ may dwell in your hearts through faith; and that you, being rooted and grounded in love, may be able to comprehend with all the saints what is the width and length and height and depth, and to know the love of Christ which surpasses knowledge, that you may be filled to all the fullness of God. Now to Him who is able to do far more abundantly beyond all that we ask or think, according to the power that works within us, to Him be the glory in the church and in Christ Jesus to all generations."*

The Lord God Almighty is so in love with mankind that He willingly shares His glory with us and no other living creation. This is an amazing concept, so bear with me. Isaiah 42:8 states that God does not share His glory, so this has stunted some people's understanding. What it actually says is, "*I am the Lord, that is My name; I will not give My glory to another, nor My praise to idols.*" The Lord will not share His glory or praise with idols, including idolaters [those who worship idols].

Romans 8:17 states, "*and if children, heirs also, heirs of God and fellow heirs with Christ, if indeed we suffer with Him so that we may also be glorified with Him.*" John 17:22 reads, "*The glory which You have given Me I also have given to them, so that they may be one, just as We are one.*"

When the Father sent the Son to Earth to die for lowly mankind [dust], He left behind His Spirit when He ascended to Heaven. When someone receives Christ, they gain the Father, Son, and Holy Spirit.

The Spirit takes residence within that person. In so doing, because we die to ourselves, Jesus' life becomes our own. In this, His glory is made manifest through us since we become one with the Son as He is one with the Father in Heaven. We become sons of God after The Son because The Son overtakes our person, spirit to Spirit.

The Father did this for the undeserving: He gave us Himself, His essence, His character, and every good gift from above. What more could we ask of Him? Nothing! His eternal love was poured onto all mankind through His shed blood. All He requires of us is to relinquish our earthly, fleshly, Adamic, tainted, corruptible, temporal life. In light of God, that is nothing much at all—astounding!

God graciously is all things to all His people. He comes to us as a father, husband, friend, brother, king, teacher, and servant, to name a few. How great a love that the Almighty of Heaven and Earth would humble Himself to be exactly what we need and when! The following are a few Scripture references to some roles.

**Father:**

"what we have seen and heard we proclaim to you also, so that you too many have fellowship with us; and indeed our fellowship is with the Father, and with His Son Jesus Christ (Isaiah 64:7)."

"See how great a love the Father has given us, that we would be called children of God (I John 3:1)."

"Do not be afraid, little flock, because your Father has chosen to give you the Kingdom (Luke 12:32)."

**Husband:**

"For your husband is your Maker, whose name is the Lord of armies…(Isaiah 54:5)."

"And it will come about on that day," declares the Lord, "that you will call Me my husband…I will betroth you to Me forever; yes, I will betroth you to Me in righteousness and in justice, in favor and in compassion (Hosea 2:16,19)."

"For I am jealous for you with a godly jealousy; for I betrothed you to one husband, to present you as a pure virgin to Christ (II Corinthians 11:2)."

"…Come, I will show you the Bride, the wife of the Lamb (Revelation 21:9)."

**Friend:**

"So the Lord used to speak to Moses face to face, just as a man speaks to his friend…(Exodus 33:11)."

"...I have called you friends, for all that I have heard from My Father I have made known to you (I John 15:15)."

"And the Scripture was fulfilled that says, 'Abraham believed God, and it was counted to him as righteousness'—and he was called a friend of God (James 2:23)."

**Brother:**

"For those whom he foreknew, He also predestined to become conformed to the image of His Son, so that He would be the firstborn among many brothers and sisters (Romans 8:29)."

"For both He who sanctifies and those who are sanctified are all from one Father; for this reason He is not ashamed to call them brothers and sisters, saying, "I will proclaim Your name to My brothers, in the midst of the assembly I will sing Your praise… Therefore, in all things, He had to be made like His brothers so that He might become a merciful and faithful high priest in things pertaining to God, to make propitiation for the sins of the people (Hebrews 2:11-12, 17)."

## Savior:

"who gave Himself for us to redeem us from every lawless deed, and to purify for Himself a people for His own possession, eager for good deeds (Titus 2:14)."

"Now having been freed from sin and enslaved to God, you derive you benefit, resulting in sanctification, and the outcome, eternal life (Romans 6:22)."

## King:

He is clothed with a robe dipped in blood, and His name is called The Word of God. And the armies which are in Heaven, clothed in fine linen, white and clean, were following Him on white horses. From His mouth comes a sharp sword, so that with it He may strike down the nations, and He will rule them with a rod of iron; and He treads the wine press of the fierce wrath of God, the almighty. And on His robe and on His thigh, He has a name written: "KING OF KINGS AND LORD OF LORDS (Revelation 19:13,16)."

"which He brought about in Christ, when He raised Him from the dead and seated Him at His right hand in the heavenly places, far above all rule and authority and power and dominion, and every name that is named, not only in this age but also in the one to come (Ephesians 1:20-21)."

**Servant:**

Then, when He had washed their feet, and taken His garments and reclined at the table again, he said to them, "Do you know what I have done for you? You call Me 'Teacher' and 'Lord'; and you are correct, for so I am. So, if I, the Lord and the Teacher, washed your feet, you also ought to wash one another's feet. For I gave you an example, so that you also would do just as I did for you (John 13:12-15)."

"Then he poured water into the basin and began washing the disciples' feet and wiping them with the towel which He had tied around Himself (John 13:5)."

"And sitting down, He called the twelve and said to them, 'If anyone wants to be first, he shall be last of all and servant of all (Mark 9:35).'"

**Teacher:**

"Now after John was taken into custody, Jesus came into Galilee, preaching [teaching] the gospel of God, and saying, 'The time is fulfilled, and the Kingdom of God has come near; repent and believe in the gospel (Mark 1:14-15)."

"…they said to Him, 'Rabbi (which translated means Teacher)…(John 1:38).'"

Matthew 5 (all)

**Shepherd:**

"The Lord is my shepherd, I will not be in need. He lets me lie down in green pastures; he leads me beside quiet waters. He restores my soul; He guides me in the paths of righteousness for His name's sake (Psalm 23:1-3)."

"I am the Good Shepherd; the Good Shepherd lays down His life for His sheep (John 10:11)."

**Comforter:**

"But the Comforter, which is the Holy Ghost, whom the Father will send in My name…(John 14:26)."

"But when the Comforter is come…(John 15:26)."

## Notes

CHAPTER TWO

# What His Love Accomplished for Mankind

But He was pierced for our offenses, He was crushed for our wrongdoings; the punishment for our well-being was laid upon Him, and by His wounds we are healed. All of us, like sheep, have gone astray, each of us has turned to his own way; but the Lord has caused the wrongdoing of us all to fall on Him. He was oppressed and afflicted, yet He did not open His mouth; like a lamb that is led to the slaughter, and like a sheep that is silent before its shearers, so He did not open His mouth. By oppression and judgment He was taken away; and as for His generation, who considered that He was cut off from the land of the living for the wrongdoing of my people, to whom the blow was due (Psalm 53:5-8).

Psalm 53 above pretty much says it all. He literally took upon Himself the suffering due to all mankind for every generation. Every time I read through these texts, I get teary-eyed and somber. There is no way anyone can possibly fully comprehend the depth of the Lord's loving mercy for us. Everything He endured for us should have happened to us and more. Anyone who has watched The Passion of the Christ by Mel Gibson may be able to somewhat visualize it. It was hard for me. What's worse is that the movie's depiction is nothing compared to what really transpired at the crucifixion.

But what does it all mean? What did Christ really accomplish? Did He merely remove sin's punishment? What exactly did He do to accomplish sin's removal from us?

Zephaniah 9:9 states, *"Rejoice greatly, daughter of Zion! Shout in triumph, daughter of Jerusalem! Behold, your king is coming to you; He is righteous and endowed with salvation, humble, and mounted on a donkey, even on a colt, the foal of a donkey."*

*"Now this expression, 'He ascended,' what does it mean except that He also had descended into the lower parts of the Earth? He who descended is Himself also He who ascended far above all the heavens, so that He might fill all things,"* reads Ephesians 4:9-10.

Hebrews 4:14 says, *"Therefore, since we have a great high priest who has passed through the heavens…,"* indicating He transcended the highest places in existence.

Did Christ enter eternal Hell for us, enduring that agony of fire and brimstone for us? Yes, He paid the ultimate price for sin's death penalty. Christ exceeded the highest and lowest places in existence—Heaven and Hell. He covered every part of everything He created to fill it all. In this *"filling,"* there is nowhere mankind can go to escape His love or righteous right hand. Isaiah 59:1 emphasizes this point, stating, *"Behold, the Lord's hand is not so short that it cannot save; nor is His ear so dull that it cannot hear."*

Jesus passed through all existence, including Sheol [the temporary place of the dead]. There is nothing anywhere He did not conquer with His love. *"But God raised Him from the dead, putting an end to the agony of death, since it was impossible for Him to be held in its power,"* says Acts 2:24. Jesus removed the sting of death and eternal torment for everyone—though not everyone will receive this incredible gift of life.

Those who die faithful to the Lord enter Paradise [Abraham's bosom], which is located in Sheol [Hades]. Those who die unfaithful to the Lord also enter Sheol. There is a debate as to whether Christ entered only Hades [a temporary holding place for the dead] or Hell [the final destination for those who rejected God].

All I know is that Christ went everywhere to fill everything. I believe Ephesians 4:9 directs us to Christ having entered and exited eternal Hell. Christ exerted

His power over all things, living and dead, powers and principalities, and evils of darkness. *"When He had disarmed the rulers and authorities, He made a public display of them, having triumphed over them through Him,"* is written in Colossians 2:15. *"Rulers and authorities"* references spiritual forces [demons and Satan; powers of darkness].

Furthermore, I Peter 3:9 states, *"not returning evil for evil or insult for insult but giving a blessing instead; for you were called for the very purpose that you would inherit a blessing."* Christ willingly paved the way for God's people to live the Father's instructions. Since Christ did not return evil for evil or insults for insults, and He becomes our life upon repentance and reception of Him, He becomes our overcoming power force from within. Because He did it then, He equips mankind to do it via Holy Spirit's power.

Finally, Matthew 27:51 reads, *"And behold, the veil of the temple was torn in two from top to bottom; and the Earth shook and the rocks were split."* Christ physically split in half the temple veil from top to bottom instead of bottom to top. In this, no human could possibly take credit for His supernatural act. Spiritually today, splitting the veil represents removing anything that would separate mankind from God. It is up to us to receive that gift of integrating Earth and Heaven.

# Notes

# CHAPTER THREE

# The Wedge Between Us and God's Love

> "For I am convinced that neither death, nor life, nor angels, nor principalities, nor things present, nor things to come, nor powers, nor height, nor depth, nor any other created thing will be able to separate us from the love of God that is in Christ Jesus our Lord (Romans 8:38-39)."

> "But your wrongdoings have caused a separation between you and your God, and your sins have hidden His face from you so that He does not hear (Isaiah 59:2)."

Looking around Christ's body, I see too many people not walking in love. For some, it is because they had a poor fatherly example or none at all. This becomes problematic when we compare God and His eternal, unfailing love to mere mortal love, which is limited, conditional, and ever-failing. For others, someone hurt them in some capacity, and their wounds seem too deep for healing to penetrate.

"*Nothing can separate us from God's love*" does not mean we never have barriers standing between us. Even with seemingly impenetrable spiritual walls, He loves us when we cannot feel or sense it. He loves us whether we are wayward, faithless, or turn our backs on Him. His love is immovable. The problem we face, then, is us. Our sin nature hides God's face, deafens His hearing, and blocks His presence.

Regardless of why one does not experience God's love, the wedge must be removed by a skilled surgeon—Jesus. The barrier between a loving God and helpless mankind must be abolished, and Jesus is the only solution. As we read in the last chapter, Christ supernaturally tore the veil from top to bottom. This requires God's people to look deeply into God's Word [Jesus in written form] and allow Holy Spirit to break the barriers that have long blocked our hearts.

Far too many people have been violated in countless ways: rape, molestation, incest, physical, mental, and/or emotional abuse, abandonment, betrayal, theft, etc. People have been laid bare, exposed to many injustices, and feel so vulnerable that nothing can break through. They opened themselves once, twice, or many times only to be crushed in soul and spirit. Even when these folks accept Christ as Savior, they commonly remain in the side effects of their abuse. They simply cannot fathom being loved by any human, much less God, the Creator of Heaven and Earth.

So how might one push past the pain and hurt to position themselves to receive God's merciful love? Honestly, it is different for everyone; there is no one way to Jesus. However, surrendering to Jesus is the only path to the loving Father. For everyone, it is truly a leap of faith with or without past trauma. Faith in Jesus is the only way, and most refuse to release themselves fully unto the Son of God. But it doesn't have to be this way.

When individuals within the body of Christ choose to seek and find their inner healing, they become catalysts for others to recognize Jesus and His healing touch. Many people grow weary of seeking such surrender and relent before an authentic, fulfilling healing and relationship with the Lord can occur.

# Notes

## CHAPTER FOUR

## My Selfless Praying Father

I will be brief here because I have written about my previous marriage debacles in my autobiography and other books. For more information, consider my books <u>Wrecked by My Ex</u>, <u>Gauchos, God, and Great Expectations</u>, or <u>How To Get It Right: Being Single, Married, Divorced, and Everything in Between</u>.

I happen to have a father who loves me unconditionally. Having endured great suffering from my first marriage resulting in entering a second marriage haphazardly. My parents stopped speaking to me for a season after I left my second husband. They were fed up with my erratic, excessively emotional, unpredictable, and inexplicable behavior contrary to who they had raised and known before marital failures that wounded me to my core.

My seven-year wilderness began in June 1993 when my first husband left a note on the coffee table. I was angry with God, my parents, and the general Christian population. Regardless, I feebly attempted to live a "*normal Christian life*," whatever that is. Once I left my second husband toward the close of 1997 in utter distress, I could not recognize myself, so things got hairy, to say the least.

It was unthinkable for my parents to stop speaking to me. We were very close, and I had no idea how to handle or remedy the situation. I was devastated. The more I attempted to fix things, the worse they grew; I tried using my fleshly, limited power instead of surrendering to the Lord. I did not seek His face and nature to guide me down the righteous path. Unfortunately, it took seven long, arduous years to realize my error.

In February 2000, I fell on my face before the Lord of Hosts, repented, surrendered, relented my selfishness, and cried out in humility to a loving, merciful, gracious God who was awaiting my return those seven years. So, what happened to lead me back to Christ? Many things, but the most significant was my selfless praying father. I have not written this in any other book, not even my autobiography, which seemed odd once I realized I had forgotten to add it. Honestly, it is one of the most monumental gifts from God. I believe it "*slipped my mind*" because God reserved it in me for such a time as this.

Also in February 2000, I met my soon-to-be mentor—we'll call her Gem—when I met with our pastor. It is only through her experience with my dad that I have knowledge of this occurrence. I couldn't be more grateful to have it!

Gem, my parents, and I all attended the same church. My dad was a long-time deacon. Every Sunday morning, the deacons and Gem would gather in the prayer room before service. According to her account, my dad did not miss a Sunday to plead, "*Pray for my daughter, Terri* [my previous name before legally becoming Alexys in January 2000]." According to her, she was undone and sick, sick, sick of praying for Terri—I'm almost sure she was being humorous!

Week after week, month after month, year after year, my faithful praying father cried out to God on my behalf. He incited others to do the same whether they wanted to or not! Of course, I was completely unaware of this. Yet, in the spirit realm, I believe I could feel them, though I didn't know what I was sensing. I was pretty oblivious in many ways, caught in my dysfunction, bitterness, anger, and chaos.

The oddest thing is that I was born-again in November 1974, at age six. I remember it vividly and meant it as much as a six-year-old is capable. I served the Lord as faithfully as I knew how throughout my upbringing. Few kids wanted to hang with me, but they always wanted me when they needed spiritual guidance or help with a school project. I always loved the Lord. To my dismay, I had no idea how lacking my spiritual life was until everything fell apart. Though the anger and sorrow persisted, I continually longed to return to the Lord.

From 1993 to 1999, I was wayward but never lost sight of God or that I needed something to help me back to Him. I did something significantly foolish toward the close of 1999. It hurt many people, including myself. That was the straw that broke the proverbial camel's back. I began praying and really seeking the Lord. It was as though I had never known the Lord because I was in such internal turmoil. Broken, wounded, and battered, I finally cried out to God on my bedroom floor, saying (paraphrased), "*Lord, I am so sick of myself and the mess I have made. Please, show me who You are! The church way did not work. The world's way did not work. There must be more to You. Please, reveal Yourself to me. Help me!*"

No one can ever convince me the Lord God Almighty did not hear and answer my dad's pleas for his daughter. In His response, He graciously sent God-fearing believers across my path in numerous ways. I am a muralist. When folks would commission me for artwork, they would often be Christians who recognized my spiritual deficit. They spoke Christ's life and love into me in the softest ways. My church family had utterly rejected me, save only two godly couples. The rest of the church folks shunned and mocked me due to my sinful behavior, never asking, "*What's wrong? How can I help?*" as true believers ought. Those two couples saw my need and helped. They, too, were answers to my father's cry.

I convey this story to depict a good father's love. I will reveal how our heavenly Father's love is superior to and far exceeds my dad's great love. And if you read this and experience irritation or sadness that you did not have this type of father, keep reading! God is a father to the fatherless, and it is revealed in His holy Word. We will cover this subject later.

# MY SELFLESS PRAYING FATHER

# IF IT WEREN'T FOR THE LOVE OF GOD

## Notes

CHAPTER FIVE

# Experiencing God's Love

I will never forget my first visible sign of God's love toward me while in rebellion. In 1998, while angrily rebelling against the Lord, I vocalized my disdain. Physically shaking my fist in the air toward Heaven in despair, I told God point blank, "*I do not doubt my salvation. I do, however, doubt the One who gave it. If You exist, I'm saved. If You don't, it doesn't matter.*" I exclaimed further, "*If You're real, show Yourself!*"

At that time, I had recently left my second husband. I lived in an apartment with a roommate, and my share of the rent was $240. How hard could it be to come up with that? I was the typical struggling artist. One month, I didn't have so much as a wooden nickel to my name, and my rent was due in a couple of days. As a new muralist on the market, my clientele was minimal.

A few days after ranting to God, a man called, explaining he needed me to paint a faux finishe the next day. I was only charging a nominal fee at the time. At the job's completion, his bill was $190. No one had ever tipped me up to that point. The man wrote a check for $240 the day before my rent was due.

When I looked at the check, I knew my Creator had shown Himself all too real. All doubt was erased in an instant. As one would imagine, I did not surrender all that moment. Still, it was the beginning of experiencing His heart of love and hand of mercy upon my life. This example is only one of countless manifestations of His unfathomable love.

## He Loved; Therefore, He Gave:

> "I permitted Myself to be sought by those who did not ask for Me; I permitted Myself to be found by those who did not seek Me. I said, 'Here am I, here am I,' to a nation which did not call on My name. I have spread out My hands all day long to a rebellious people, who walk in the way which is not good, following their thoughts, a people who continually provoke Me to My face (Isaiah 65:1-2)."

For God so loved the world that He gave (John 3:16). This statement sets the tone for God's entire Word. He loved; therefore, He gave. Encountering countless people from varying denominations and backgrounds,

I have discovered the most significant problem among the body of Christ—few know that God is deeply and irreversibly in love with them. By "*know*," I mean concretely burrowed in the deepest part of their being [their spirit] not simply "*have some knowledge of.*"

If we knew, if we really knew, we would not allow our flesh to remain in control another moment. This would mean we would not tolerate pride on any level because we would understand He rejects the prideful. We would cease reacting in anger, greed, malice, prejudice, hatred, perversion, or anything of the like because Christ's love would operate 24/7/365 in and through us. Generally speaking, God's people don't know how to love because, quite frankly, they don't know He loves them, or at least they don't understand the magnitude of His love or how to receive it fully.

Oh, Christians talk a good game, sing lovely songs, and look as though they perpetually delight in God's love. But, at their base, they have little concept of His eternal love. This is why few people have been able to see The Way [Christ] in the fall of Adam. People ask angrily, "*If God is so perfect and all-knowing, why did He create Adam and Eve knowing what would happen?*" In a nutshell, they are asking, "*What is God's problem? Is He stupid? Is He imperfect? Is He really loving?*" These people shake their spiritual fists at Him, demanding correction as if He is errant. People grow irritated with me when I speak so candidly, but I genuinely believe it is past time to get honest with ourselves and God to begin healing from the inside out.

When we begin crying out to the Almighty, asking Him to reveal the height, width, depth, and length of His love, we open the door, allowing Him to unveil our eyes to see as He sees, our ears to hear as He hears, and our minds to think as He thinks. Because of His love, He had to create Adam, and yes, let Adam die so all mankind who willingly choose His death might live eternally and abundantly in Him, with Him, and through Him. He doesn't need us, but He longingly wants us. There is no earthly love source to which we can adequately compare His love.

He earnestly desires us to reciprocally long for Him. The greatest command is to love the Lord our God with all our hearts, souls, minds, and strength. The second is to love our neighbor as ourselves. Aside from God's love, there is nothing. His love in us allows us to love our neighbor, even if they are our enemy. This same love allows His Spirit to live in and operate through our spirits. It is this love that says, "*Die so that I may fill you with My fullness so you may share in My divine nature.*" It is because of His love for mankind that we are called to die to self. Death ushers a better life, a new divine eternal life far beyond anything of the life we know aside from Christ.

We should ask for our spirits to be quickened, allowing us to walk in His merciful, compassionate love. Have you ever been in a relationship where you served someone from obligation but didn't want to? Or have you ever been in a relationship with someone you loved so dearly that you couldn't wait to serve them because you long to please them?

It is one thing to serve God from duty, and many do. It is another to serve Him because we are head over heels in love with Him. People tend to perceive God as a boss instead of a lover. I am in love with Yahweh in this way, and I only know a few others who are. I boast not in myself but in He who transformed my thinking, seeing, hearing, and doing. It's time to stop rebelling, which includes keeping a barrier over our hearts, blocking Him from penetrating us through and through.

## Notes

CHAPTER SIX

*Eternal Life and Love*

> For it is by grace you have been saved, through faith—and this not from yourselves, it is the gift of God—not by works, so that no one can boast. For we are God's workmanship, created in Christ Jesus to do good works, which God prepared in advance for us to do (Ephesians 2:8-10).

I spent way too many years of salvation not knowing true eternal life. John 17:3-5 defines eternal life as "*knowing the Father and the Son.*" All I knew was the Son, and barely. I did not view Him as the lover of my inner-most being, longing to extend goodness to me. Salvation means to be "*rescued*" from a condemned world and Hell. Eternal life is a personal relationship allowing us to commune with God on His level through Holy Spirit. God sees the blood and Spirit of His righteous Son, not our old sinful nature. With eternal life, we are no longer an "*old dirty sinner*" but a saint because The Saint [Jesus] has overtaken us. Our nature is no longer ours as it has been transformed into something of Heaven instead of Earth.

What an intense, immense privilege to intimately know God, the Creator of all things—to make Him known, and to be known by Him. I urge everyone to check themselves. If we walk in fear, doubt, anger, bitterness, impatience, greed, jealousy, pride, indifference, etc., and deem ourselves as "*good*," eternal life may not have taken root. There is no one good but God.

## **Love, Love, Love!**

> …and perseverance, proven character; and proven character, hope; and hope does not disappoint, because the love of God has been poured out within our hearts through the Holy Spirit who was given to us…but God demonstrates His love toward us, in that while we were yet sinners, Christ died for us (Romans 5:4, 5, 8).

> "There is no fear in love; but perfect love casts out fear, because fear involves punishment, and the one who fears is not perfected in love (I John 4:18)."

> "Beyond all these things put on love, which is the perfect bond of unity (Colossians 3:14)."

The above Scriptures do not reference the conditional, shallow, limited love the flesh offers. This is pure and holy love we can only attain through the infilling of Holy Spirit via God's Son. When we sincerely ask the Father to reveal every wicked way within us, He certainly will oblige. However, it is not for condemnation (Romans 8:1) but to have the opportunity to repent so we may be set free. He disciplines us because of His great love for us, revealing life's muck and mire packed deep within.

He desires to "*share His holiness.*" How amazing is God's love?!

When He instructs us to "*die to self,*" it is not for punishment but for freedom. He longs to give us all He possesses. Yet, He cannot as long as we choose the world and its lusts, which includes the emotional and mental damage inflicted by others or ourselves. Jesus wants to romance us, to woo us to Himself. Pray for Him to plow up the fallowed ground built around your heart (Jeremiah 4:3-4). Pray for His Word, the Sword of the Spirit, to divide your soul from your spirit so your spirit may become alive to commune with Him on a most intimate level.

Head-knowledge alone means nothing. Heart knowledge alone means nothing. I have encountered multitudes who go through charismatic motions yet are not walking in love. They seem to be charismatic for the sake of being charismatic. If a believer is charismatic, charisma should result from being in love with the Lord, and they cannot help themselves.

If a person is in a relationship and starts feeling like they want to get out but don't know how, they bide their time, pretending to be in love. The affection is forced and eventually disappears. However, when a person is genuinely, intensely, irreversibly in love, they can't constrain themselves from having charisma for that person or stop themselves from talking about and doing for their love interest.

Many people have all the necessary information from God's Word and even spend much time reading it, but they lack oneness [unity] with God, which is essential to supernaturally comprehend or operate in His love. The Word says love is the key to unity. Plainly stated, Christ's love has not overwhelmed most people. I understand why countless denominations have forsaken such spiritual gifts as the apostolic, prophetic, healing, and speaking in tongues. On the flipside, I dare say that in my personal experience, most who operate in spiritual gifts do so while lacking Christ's love. They function in their gifts because it is the "*religious*" or "*right*" thing to do. It allows them to be accepted by those around them but is superficial, or at best, obligatory.

The prophet, specifically, struggles with a lack of love. How many cruel prophets have I encountered? Many! They seem to have the idea prophets must be harsh to be effective. I know firsthand the prophet's role is often to bring a word of correction. Yet, if it does not come with God's love at its core to turn a person to repentance, it is not only meaningless but harmful to a severe degree. Truth in love is God's way. Even a difficult word to hear should be spoken with love at the root.

Eternal life, on Earth or in Heaven, is about love. No matter where we are, what we say or do, or what has been done to us, God's love must be our driving force. Colossians 3:23-24 teaches us, *"Whatever you do, do your work heartily, as for the Lord and not for people, knowing that it is from the lord that you will receive the reward of the inheritance. It is the Lord Christ whom you serve."*

# Notes

CHAPTER SEVEN

# I Am Nothing Without Love

> "If I speak with the tongues of men and of angels, but do not have love, I have become a noisy gong or a clanging cymbal. If I have the gift of prophecy and know all mysteries and all knowledge; and if I have all faith, to remove mountains, but do not have love, I am nothing (I Corinthians 13:1-2)."

God's anointed should be in harmonious sync with His Kingdom as opposed to that of a clanging cymbal. By self-checking our walk with the Trinity, if we find He is not the love of our lives, we are not Holy Spirit-led. It is impossible to be because the flesh is still active. It may not be evident to all, but it is to God. He is the only One to whom we ultimately answer. We are to be God-pleasers, not people-pleasers.

We need to die to ourselves [consider our old nature as dead], obsessed with and possessed by Holy Spirit. Many fault me for speaking so boldly and drawing such a definitive line. They argue that this is too extreme, and I should not put that kind of pressure on people. Regardless, without understanding the line to which God calls His people, we will fail in every way.

Only the Spirit of God through us can produce eternal fruit. Whatever good deeds we produce in our limited flesh is as nothing because it is limited and only of self. Absolute submission is the only authentic submission. It stems from a heart filled with the love of and for Christ Jesus. Total submission is without pressure because death can't feel pressure, or anything else for that matter. Partial submission is rebellion against our Holy Lord God.

No amount of reading the Bible can help us if we are not reading to seek and find. The words will seem void and meaningless because only He can reveal His Word. Intellect does not bring one to Christ. Humble hearts, willing to surrender, do. Pray before reading. Seek to hear His voice and to identify His love behind the words.

## Trials Are Revealing:

> "so that the proof of your faith, being more precious than gold which is perishable, even though tested by fire, may be found to result in praise and glory and honor at the revelation of Jesus Christ (I Peter 1:7)."

> "If you do well, will not your countenance be lifted up? And if you do not do well, sin is crouching at the door; and its desire is for you, but you must master it (Genesis 4:7)."

If I have heard once, I have heard a thousand times, *"They were such a good person until thus and so happened. Then they changed for the worse."* With all of my being, I believe trials and tests do not change a person but rather bring to light what someone is at their core. It was true in Job's case as well as mine. Neither of us knew the wickedness of our hearts until disasters came. As Matthew 12:34 says, *"…for the mouth speaks from that which fills the heart."* Trying times reveal our heart's true thoughts, intentions, and feelings.

Adam lived in a utopia, and it was true for him. The worst comes from people in dire situations because the love of Christ was not truly in effect. Sure, they may be saved from Hell, but a person led by Holy Spirit would be able to recognize what God was allowing to happen instead of blowing up from losing sight of reality. Just because Holy Spirit leads someone for a long time does not mean they cannot instantly revert to a fleshly mindset. Satan is crouching at the door, waiting for an opportunity to stumble us. You and I must daily die, which is merely a result of having been transformed into God's image.

# I AM NOTHING WITHOUT LOVE

When my first husband left, I fell apart. I began cursing, ranting, and raving. Why? It was because I had no grounding in an intimate relationship with God. I had never once said, "*Father, show me everything wrong within me. Lead me into righteousness.*" I had received salvation as a little child and went on my way "*getting people saved*" [from Hell] as I was taught. I didn't drink, curse, sleep around, or do drugs. I was a "*good*" kid. However, it was basically a façade because no one is truly good but God.

I failed to know how to hear from God, receive warnings, corrections, or anything of the kind. If I could have, I would not have married two wrong men. I knew nothing of God except the ability to quote a few Scriptures and how to avoid Hell. In my mind, making a profession of faith was equated as "*an intimate relationship*" when it was merely the beginning of what should have developed into an intimate relationship.

God is so intensely in love with the human race that He prolongs His return. Given the magnitude of personal and global turmoil, many grow irritated that Christ has not returned. As a whole, the body of Christ wants a scapegoat with the rapture—I hear it all the time. Christ's bride would prefer to selfishly welcome the rapture than get cleaned and complete her Kingdom assignment on Earth as God intends, ushering, "*May it be on Earth as it is in Heaven.*"

Every Christ-follower's mission statement should be the same as Christ's, "*To live in Holy Spirit anointing, preaching the gospel to the poor, proclaiming release to the captives and recovery of sight to the blind; setting free those who are oppressed, and proclaiming the favorable year of the Lord* (Luke 4:18-19)."

To God's deep chagrin, the bulk of Christ's body is too lazy and self-absorbed to seek this. The Word says He tarries because of His patience, not desiring that any should perish (II Peter 3:9). The root problem is the lack of love—His pure, holy, unblemished love. If we loved the lost as He, we would not long for His return as much as concerning ourselves with setting free those still in sin's captivity. The lack of His love leaves one selfish and cold.

May the body of Christ hasten to walk the straight and narrow path so she may be a light in this dark and dying world, to beckon the height, width, length, and depth of His love, and proclaim it over God's bride with boldness. Begin to personally, intimately love Him with all your heart, soul, mind, and strength. Stop the ritualistic motions. Seek God for a Kingdom mindset. Get cleaned like David, so we all may be able to pray for God to search the inmost parts of our beings only to find no iniquity. Purity is freedom, so the lost will supernaturally be drawn into the love they see through you and me.

# Notes

CHAPTER EIGHT

# God's Loving Discipline

Thus, you are to know in your heart that the Lord your God was disciplining you just as a man disciplines his son. Therefore, you shall keep the commandments of the Lord your God, to walk in His ways and to fear Him. For the Lord your God is bringing you into a good land…in which you will not lack anything… when you have eaten and are satisfied, you shall bless the Lord your God for the good land which He has given you (Deuteronomy 8:5-10).

"Blessed is the man who perseveres under trial; for once he has been approved, he will receive the crown of life which the Lord has promised to those who love Him (James 1:12)."

He will increase our territory when we prove our devotion to Him through discipline and testing. What we already have will expand. If we do not obey, what we have will be recalled. Many want God to remove their trials and tribulations, but He would not call us to live victoriously if there was nothing to conquer. Victory is a product of battle. If there was nothing to overcome, there would be no purpose for us to remain on Earth post-salvation. No tribulations = no victory = no testimony = the lost will remain lost.

Testing reveals wickedness that remains in us; it teaches us how to confess and repent, how to allow Him to shake out of us whatever is not planted by and secured in the Rock of Salvation, how to stretch our faith in Him as He proves Himself worthy to be praised, and how to grow our love for the Lord as He shows Himself real in, through, and for us. Through testing, the desired goal is to bring us into a deeper place of humility after realizing we are nothing, in and of ourselves, but He in us is everything. Trials instill a higher level of obedience through learning how to become disciplined in all our ways. They reveal the heart and love of God. When struggles ensue, God's love is available to those who humble themselves to receive all He has awaiting us. Again, God's love is nothing like man's feeble attempt at love.

## God's Love Toward Us:

> "See how great a love the Father has bestowed on us, that we would be called children of God…(I John 3:1)."

> "For the Scripture says, 'Whoever believes in Him will not be disappointed (Romans 10:11).'"

> "For I am convinced that neither death, nor life, nor angels, nor principalities, nor things present, nor things to come, nor powers, not height, nor depth, nor any other created thing, will be able to separate us from the love of God…(Romans 8:38-39)."

There is nothing God won't give to those who love Him, fear Him, and keep His commands. Of course, because we live in an earthen vessel, the vessel itself is tainted, so He looks upon Holy Spirit within. His love never fails, and we are never separated from His love. Sin separates us from the blessings and presence, which is different from being separated from His love.

This is why sin is sin in God's eye [single vision]. He died for all sin and all sinners for all time. Individual acts of sin halt the flow of blessings in our lives. The more significant the sin, the harder to overcome, the more difficult to repent, the longer it goes unconfessed, the longer we wallow in filth, the longer we sow bad seed, the longer we must reap a bad harvest. Understanding the difference between being separated from His love [impossible] and being separated from His covenant blessings and presence [possible] is crucial to a successful life in Christ.

God's love is unfailing. His blessings are contingent upon our level of obedience and love. Many verses read, "*...in that area of your life, it will go well with you.*" This is why many "*love*" God but only experience victory in certain life areas. We can be obedient in honoring our parents and be blessed with children that honor us. On the other hand, that same person may disrespect their husband or not purely love their wife, so their marriage does not go well.

In other words, the blessings will always fall upon the areas where we are obedient but not in the areas of disobedience. This is why we must always be aware of not only the promises of God but the commands to which they are attached. The more areas of obedience, the more the blessings will abound. The less compliance, the lesser the blessings.

As an aside, "*blessings*" are not tangible objects. Authentic Kingdom blessings are peace, joy, and love amid turbulent circumstances. Any physical blessing is secondary. Deuteronomy 7 states we are a "*holy people.*" We must purpose in our hearts to conduct ourselves as holy people instead of merely "*old dirty rotten sinners.*"

# Notes

CHAPTER NINE

## How Does God See Love?

So, as those who have been chosen of God, holy and beloved, put on a heart of compassion, kindness, humility, gentleness, and patience; bearing with one another, and forgiving each other, whoever has a complaint against anyone; just as the Lord forgave you, so must you do also. In addition to all these things put on love, which is the perfect bond of unity (Colossians 3:12-14).

**Walk of Love:**

Proper application of knowledge and understanding is crucial to life. They are vital to us becoming stable in all our ways and increasing in our Christ identity. True knowledge is intimacy with God, not just endless data. Knowledge is a scary thing in the hands of a natural-thinking man. Man likes to puff himself when they feel they know a thing or two about anything. The knowledge of God confounds the knowledge of man. Genuinely knowledgeable people do not see themselves as such. I Corinthians 8:1 reveals, "... *knowledge makes one conceited, but love edifies people."*

For example, I know the Word—I am in love with the Word. Some know the Word less, and some more. If I compare myself with those who know less, I will become boastful in my knowledge. If I compare myself with those who know more, I will become ashamed of my lack. Shame is a manifestation of pride because it is rooted in and focused on self instead of God. Any time self is our focus, pride is afoot. The bottom line is that pride takes root when I compare myself to anyone, causing my eventual demise. There is no love in playing the *"who is better than who"* game.

Knowing this truth, I compare my knowledge only with the depth of God's knowledge. He is all-knowing. Compared to Him, I know nothing. This way, I constantly desire to learn and grow without thinking more highly of myself than I ought. My only focus is to love and please the Lord unconditionally. Being in love with Yeshua ushers His knowledge, humility, and understanding. Love is the ultimate ticket to everything God.

*"Jesus Christ is the same yesterday, today, and forever,"* reads Hebrews 13:8. Neither His promises nor His stipulations change. He calls us to love as He loves. Above all, our walk with Christ must be one of love, the Father's authentic supernatural

love. Earthly, human love is defiled and worthless in the grand scheme. Outside of Christ, our love is condemned, limited, and conditional. God's love, adversely, is unlimited, eternal, without measure, and unconditional. To claim God's promises, we must walk like Jesus. God will test us to reveal how much we love and trust Him.

## Requirements for Blessings:

> "We know that God causes all things to work together for good to those who love God, to those who are called according to His purpose (Romans 8:28)."

> "But Joseph said to them, "Do not be afraid, for am I in God's place? As for you, you meant evil against me, but God meant it for good… (Genesis 50:19-20)."

> "Now it shall be, if you diligently obey the Lord your God, being careful to do all His commandments which I command you today, the Lord your God will set you high above all the nations of the Earth. All the following blessings will come upon you and overtake you *if* you obey the Lord your God:
>
>   1. Blessed shall you be in the city, and in the country

2. Blessed shall be the offspring of your body and the produce of your ground and the offspring of your beasts, the increase of your herd and the young of your flock
3. Blessed shall be your basket and your kneading bowl
4. Blessed shall you be when you come in, and when you go out
5. The Lord shall cause your enemies who rise up against you to be defeated before you; they will come out against you one way and will flee before you in seven ways
6. The Lord will command the blessing upon you in your barns and in all that you put your hand to, and He will bless you in the land which the Lord your God gives you
7. The Lord will establish you as a holy people to Himself, as He swore to you
8. All the peoples of the Earth will see that you are called by the name of the Lord, and they will be afraid of you
9. The Lord will make you abound in prosperity, in the offspring of your body and in the offspring of your beast and in the produce of your ground, in

the land which the Lord swore to your fathers to give you
10. The Lord will open for you His good storehouse, the heavens, to give rain to your land in its season and to bless all the work of your hand; and you shall lend to many nations, but you shall not borrow
11. The Lord will make you the head and not the tail, and you only will be above, and you will not be underneath, if you listen to the commandments of the Lord your God (Deuteronomy 28:1-14).

God Almighty is the quintessential Giver. The texts above are all guarantees for God's obedient people. We have the privilege of claiming them in any dire situation. However, I must reiterate that to be a recipient, obedience is mandatory. Many of God's people attempt to claim the blessed promises without personal obedience to His commands. His command, above all else, is love. God views mankind's love as obedience to His will and purpose.

Understand that all things working together for good are contingent upon our love for Jesus, not His love for us. His love is already perfect and complete, and He cannot love us any more than He already does. We must step in accordance to love for Him to take what Satan means against us for evil and turn it around for good.

When we walk in a condition of love toward God, as Satan comes against us with any trial, we can boldly claim that God has already turned it around for our good in the spirit realm. We must patiently await and call forth its manifestation. God sees love as noted in Galatians 5:22: love, joy, peace, patience, kindness, goodness, gentleness, and self-control.

# Notes

**CHAPTER TEN**

# Love Your Enemy as Your Neighbor

You have heard that it was said, 'You shall love your neighbor and hate your enemy.' But I say to you, love your enemies and pray for those who persecute you, so that you may be sons of your Father who is in Heaven; for He causes His sun to rise on the evil and the good, and sends rain on the righteous and the unrighteous. For if you love those who love you, what reward do you have? Do not even the tax collectors do the same? If you greet only your brothers, what more are you doing than others? Do not even the Gentiles do the same? Therefore you are to be perfect, as your heavenly Father is perfect (Matthew 5:43-46).

"… love your enemies, do good to those who hate you, bless those who curse you, pray for those who mistreat you (Luke 6:27-28)."

Owe nothing to anyone except to love one another; for he who loves his neighbor has fulfilled the law. For this, "You shall not commit adultery, you shall not murder, you shall not steal, you shall not covet," and if there is any other commandment, it is summed up in this saying, "You shall love your neighbor as yourself." Love does no wrong to a neighbor; therefore love is the fulfillment of the law (Romans 13:8-10).

"I have been crucified with Christ; and it is no longer I who live, but Christ lives in me; and the life which I now live in the flesh I live by faith in the Son of God, who loved me and gave Himself up for me (Galatians 2:20)."

**Definition of Crucify**: put (someone) to death by nailing or binding them to a cross, especially as an ancient punishment.

**Definition of Love:**
1. a profoundly tender, passionate affection for another person.
2. a feeling of warm personal attachment or deep affection, as for a parent, child, or friend.
3. a person toward whom love is felt; beloved person; sweetheart.

4. used in direct address as a term of endearment, affection, or the like
5. a love affair; an intensely amorous incident; amour.
6. sexual intercourse; copulation

"*Love your enemies and do good*" is a God-command. Don't forget that Jesus said there is no one good but God. That being so, we cannot possibly "*do good*" lest we are led by the Author of good. That makes loving our enemy a supernatural act of God versus a natural act of man. We cannot truly love our enemy on our own, it is impossible. Only Christ's pure and perfect supernatural love flowing through us will allow our natural body to conduct itself contrary to its common character. We must submit ourselves to the Father's will. Then, and only then, will we possess the capacity to love our enemy.

Keep in mind that in the spiritual sense, we're already considered as dead since Christ buried the flesh of all mankind at His burial. "*Dying to self*" is not "*killing a dead thing*," but instead accepting daily that we are dead outside of Christ. In being "*dead*," we realize we can lend nothing to aid the cause of Christ. A dead man cannot love or hate, forgive or withhold forgiveness, and so on. A dead man can do nothing of himself. Only in the new life of Christ operating through us can we take action. In this, it isn't for us to love, but instead allow God's love to pour upon friends, family, enemies, etc. Otherwise, we will be Satan's puppet with all his vileness.

This goes back to the fact that the most oppressed people have the greatest opportunity to show God's power through their lives post-transformation. Suppose the one experiencing prejudice extends love toward their enemy. In that case, the enemy is overthrown because of God's mercy and love selflessly displayed. This is how we can claim the promise in Proverbs 6:31, *"The thief must give back seven times what he stole, even up to his entire household."*

Satan is our ultimate enemy, and the Earth is his household. There is no limit to what will be returned to us because God's promise of return is securely intact. I can give to the thief who takes from me because I know something much bigger and better from God is just over the horizon. This is an act of true faith in Christ's Word—Christ's love in action.

Knowing this promise, I can laugh at whatever comes my way, and so can we all. God laughs at the days ahead because He knows the end result (Psalm 2:4 & 37: 13). Genesis 21:6-7 shows where Sarah said God gave her laughter. How awesome! Only God's love can usher such laughter in the face of the enemy. Proverbs 31 speaks of the wife who walks upright, able to laugh at the days ahead. You and I, being merged with Christ, know the end result in every situation.

Not every detail but that we will prevail in the end. By the way, the Proverbs 31 woman is not an individual female but Christ's body [men and women of the Almighty].

We may not know exactly how it will turn, but I know it will work as an eventual benefit. When an enemy in human form steals something from me, I have no problem giving them more. I am confident in God's promise to restore unto me sevenfold. This does not exempt me from having negative feelings about a thief, but His love in me allows that love to override my fleshly emotions.

This confidence comes from knowing God is in love with me and equally that I am in love with Him. Love makes all the difference. In such love, I can easily and readily love my enemy and my neighbor as myself. It's because I realize how loved I am by God, that God is my life, and I can allow God to love Himself through me. God's supernatural, endless love flows from Heaven into my worthless body, allowing His love to bring supernatural life to and through me. In this, His love is returned to Him perfectly. In such a flow of God's love, how can I not love my neighbor as myself, even when my neighbor is my enemy?

An enemy and neighbor have a greater opportunity to receive love when it is supernaturally given through a Christ follower. That person may well come to Christ because of our selfless act of giving to the thief and loving the unlovable. We will be known by man that we are God's when we operate in the fullness of love, especially toward those who hate us. We will also be known by the demons. May Satan, his army, and all mankind testify that we walk with God, that they may not touch us because they cannot touch God living in us. Above all, may God testify of our love for Him!

If you're wondering if loving people is the same as liking people, the answer is "*NO!*" Nowhere in the Bible does God command, or even mention, liking our fellow man. Many have told me that they can only love people they like. However, that doesn't make biblical sense. If someone is my enemy, I will not like them for that reason alone! No one likes someone who stands against them and intends to harm them in some capacity.

When I was bullied throughout my school years, I did not like any of them. When my ex-husband did what he did against me all those years, I did not like him. In my seven years of rebellion against God, I did not like myself all that much—my conduct became an enemy to God and myself. "*Like*" has nothing to do with anything; it is irrelevant.

# Notes

CHAPTER ELEVEN

## God's Perfected Love

Beloved, let us love one another, for love is from God… God is love. By this the love of God was manifested in us… not that we loved God, but that He loved us and sent His Son to be the propitiation for our sins. Beloved, if God so loved us, we also ought to love one another. No one has seen God at any time; if we love one another, God abides in us, and His love is perfected in us…by this, love is perfected with us, so that we may have confidence in the day of judgment; because as He is, so also are we in this world. There is no fear in love; but perfect love casts out fear, because fear involves punishment, and the one who fears is not perfected in love. We love, because He first loved us (I John 4:7-14, 17-19).

**God's Love Perfected in Us:**

Jesus states in John 15, *"Greater love has no one than this, that one lay down his life for his friends…love one another."* Yes, Jesus is the ultimate friend, having laid down His life for us, but this also applies to you and me. We are called to lay down our lives [our fleshly man] for Christ. In so doing, He can fill our empty shell with all that is pure and holy. Being filled, we can do as God—we can love others in their sinful condition just as He loved us in ours. God's love can look past what the human eyes see and see through the single, undistracted lens of pure, complete love.

Because God first loved us in our wicked condition before we knew Him, we ought to love one another. God is love. If we are in Christ, love cannot help but pour through us. Love will no longer be a forced issue. There will always be those who are challenging to love, no doubt. That fact won't change because it is the worldly nature surrounding us. We must be transformed by renewing our minds to have our hearts and conduct altered accordingly. The new us will stop, think, and act according to love [Holy Spirit] instead of the flesh.

## Armor Provision:

> Put on the full armor of God...Buckle the belt of truth around your waist...breastplate of righteousness...boots of peace... shield of faith...helmet of salvation and the sword of the Spirit, which is the Word of God. Pray in the Spirit on all occasions with all kinds of

prayers and requests. Be alert and always keep on praying for all the saints (Ephesians 6:11-18).

For the Lord gives wisdom; from His mouth come knowledge and understanding. He stores up sound wisdom for the upright; He is a shield to those who walk in integrity, guarding the paths of justice, and He preserves the way of His Godly ones…discretion will guard you, understanding will watch over you, to deliver you from the way of evil, from the man who speaks perverse things (Proverbs 2:6-14).

"Do not let kindness and truth leave you; bind them around your neck, write them on the tablet of your heart (Proverbs 3:3)."

"…put on the Lord Jesus Christ, and make no provision for the flesh…(Romans 13:12)."

The Lord has not left us helpless, though we often feel helpless if we do not know what He has provided or how to use such provision. Everyday, we must acknowledge that with which God has armed us. Visualize the Father placing all His armor on our person. There are more pieces than what is mentioned in Ephesians. Paul says to "*Put it on, take up.*" Heed the word of God's wise apostle.

The armor allows one to stand when others around us are falling. Saying "*I put on…*" and listing the armor does not mean we are armed with the Lord. Since the armor of God is not physical, we cannot "*put it on*" like we would clothing. It is a matter of filling [arming] ourselves with the Word [studying to show ourselves approved]. It is a place of utter surrender to the Father's will. His armor is Jesus, the Father's love made manifest.

Additionally, he states, "*Pray in the Spirit always.*" This is not speaking in tongues all day, every day, contrary to popular belief. It is simply being so in tune with God's heart that we pray forth His will no matter what. Our spirit-man needs to be tapped into Holy Spirit 24/7/365, never allowing our spirit to be controlled by our soul, flesh, people, circumstances, the devil, or his demons.

Psalm 18:35 reads, "*Your gentleness…*" This means we should bind to ourselves the gentleness of Christ Jesus. We must intentionally allow all God is to be bound to us to be girded in righteousness. Proverbs speaks of wisdom, understanding, discernment, discretion, kindness, truth, and knowledge—we must bind these to ourselves, seeking them with a vengeance. Let nothing stand in the way of receiving all of God to be holy and protected in all things.

Romans 13 clearly states, *"Put on Christ."* Not a part of Him, but all.

## Whom Shall I Fear?

> "Though I walk in the midst of trouble, You will revive me; You will stretch forth Your hand against the wrath of my enemies, and Your right hand will save me. The Lord will accomplish what concerns me; Your lovingkindness, O Lord, is everlasting; do not forsake the works of Your hands (Psalm 138:7-8)."

> The Lord is my light and my salvation; whom shall I fear? The Lord is the strength of my life; of whom shall I be afraid? When the wicked, even my enemies and my foes, came upon me to eat up my flesh, they stumbled and fell. Though a host should encamp against me, my heart shall not fear; though war should rise against me, in this will I be confident (Psalm 27:1-3).

We must not allow ourselves an opportunity to be offended by the enemy. Just as God speaks through His people, Satan can also speak. If a person is speaking against us, it is demonically guided. The spirit realm is far greater than the natural—God's Word is clear on this matter. Remember, the enemy is not another human being but Satan operating through them.

Satan desires us to kill each other. God expects us to love one another, even and especially our enemies. We must arm ourselves in righteousness and love. To reiterate, Satan's goal is not to cause us to sin for the sake of sinning but to separate us from God's blessings and presence—more importantly, to divide the Kingdom of God. We know a kingdom divided against itself cannot stand—it will surely fall. If Satan can fragment God's Kingdom, we're done. Let us, God's people, stand united by recognizing the true enemy, stop fearing him and his tactics and, through loving the Lord our God, allow Him to fight our battles.

It is paramount to arm ourselves with Christ's perfect love, purpose, and mind. We must conduct ourselves as He desires to conduct Himself through our natural body. It is critical to know His goal and make it ours. His purpose is to expand His Kingdom on Earth, so likewise, our purpose is the same. God's Word is our weapon in this life. We belong on Earth, but we are not from Earth. We are from Heaven, sent from the King to rule on His behalf. This is so because Christ [of Heaven] resides in our earthen vessel, deeming us "*of Heaven*."

Since we are here for such a time, take all provision from Heaven, allowing Him to utilize His own weaponry for His good and ours. God has nothing with which to work if we don't have His Word rooted within. As I have stated in other books, God does not work with mankind but with Himself within mankind.

For all those choosing to be led by Satan refusing to submit to God, let God deal with them. That is His job. We do not need to come against those who come against us. God's wrath toward those who war against His people is far worse than anything we could do. Prayer and love are the most potent weapons we have. Cover all in prayer and let God's will, plan, and purpose arise. The enemy of God's people is His personal enemy. He contends with those who contend with His own (Psalm 35).

When we are secure in knowing who we are in Christ, we will never again fear any bad news. Perfect love casts out fear (I John 4:18). We will be unshakable. Our trust and faith in the Almighty will be untouchable. Psalm 60:4 declares boldly, *"He will have no fear of bad news; his heart is steadfast, trusting in the Lord. His heart is secure. He will have no fear; in the end, he will look in triumph on his foes."* This is God's perfect love.

*"Great peace have they which love Thy law: and nothing shall offend them,"* is found in Psalm 119:165, KJV. God's Law is Love. When we abide His Law [Love], we live in perfect peace.

# Notes

CHAPTER TWELVE

# What About the Fatherless?

This is what the Lord God says to Jerusalem: "Your origin and your birth are from the land of the Canaanite; your father was an Amorite and your mother a Hittite. As for your birth, on the day your navel cord was not cut, nor were you washed with water for cleansing; you were not rubbed with salt or even wrapped in cloths. No eye looked with pity on you to do any of these things for you, to have compassion on you. Rather you were thrown out into the open field, for you were abhorred on the day you were born. When I passed by you and saw you squirming in your blood, I said to you while you were in your blood, "Live!" Yes, I said to you while you were in your blood, "Live!" (Ezekiel 16:3-7)

"A father to the fatherless and a judge for the widows, is God in His holy dwelling (Psalm 68:5)."

> "I will not leave you as orphans; I am coming to you. After a little while, the world no longer is going to see Me, but you are going to see Me; because I live, you also will live. On that day you will know that I am in My Father, and you are in Me, and I in you. The one who has My commandments and keeps them is the one who loves Me; and the one who loves Me will be loved by My Father, and I will love him and will reveal Myself to him." Judas (not Iscariot) said to Him, "Lord, what has happened that You are going to reveal Yourself to us and not to the world?" Jesus answered and said to him, "If anyone loves Me, he will follow My Word; and My Father will love him, and We will come to him and make Our dwelling with him. The one who does not love me does not follow My words; and the word which you hear is not Mine, but the Father's who sent Me (John 14:18-24)."

Although the opening Scripture was the Word of the Lord to Ezekiel for Jerusalem [God's chosen people], this is exactly what He did for the Gentiles when He sent His Son to die and arise from the dead for all mankind. "*Gentile*" simply means "*non-Jewish.*"

The above Scriptures absolutely astound me! God's infinite love blows my frail, human mind. How can

God love those as wicked as mankind? Why can He love us? When did His love for us begin?

1. **How**: He is incapable of not loving us. (I John 4:16)
2. **Why**: because He is love. (I John 4:8)
3. **When**: before the foundation of the world. (Ephesians 1:4)

Ephesians 1:3-6 reads, "*Blessed be the God and Father of our Lord Jesus Christ, who has blessed us with every spiritual blessing in the heavenly places in Christ, just as He chose us in Him before the foundation of the world, that we would be holy and blameless before Him. In love, He predestined us to adoption as sons and daughters through Jesus Christ to Himself, according to the good pleasure of His will, to the praise of the glory of His grace, with which He favored us in the Beloved.*"

If you read the chapter about my dad and thought, "*Well, poo, I didn't have that kind of father or a father at all. I must be doomed to be fatherless with no one to pray for or help me,*" be encouraged! The Lord God is a father to the fatherless. All we need to do is allow Him to father us. He intercedes for us on a superior level than any human father could ever think or imagine. You are not an orphan, or at least you do not have to remain one. When anyone gives their life to the Lord, they are adopted as a son [male and female], an heir to God's throne and heavenly Kingdom. In fact, Jesus intercedes for you in prayer before the Father, night and day.

Hebrews 4:14-16 confirms this, stating, "*Therefore, since we have a great high priest who has passed through the heavens, Jesus the Son of God, let's hold firmly to our confession. For we do not have a high priest who cannot sympathize with our weaknesses, but One who has been tempted in all things just as we are, yet without sin. Therefore, let's approach the throne of grace with confidence, so that we may receive mercy and find grace for help at the time of our need.*" Hebrews 5:1-14 continues this train of thought. I recommend reading it.

Revelation 12 confirms the Father gave His power to Jesus while in human form, who gave the same power to those who love Him and are called according to His purpose. Verse 10 says, "…*Now the salvation and the power and the Kingdom of our God and the authority of His Christ have come, for the accuser of our brothers and sisters has been thrown down, the one who accuses them before our God day and night. And they overcame him by the blood of the Lamb* [Jesus] *and because of the word of their testimony, and they did not love their life even when faced with death*?

Though it may seem odd, I share Revelation because this is what we have all been given through Jesus' shed blood—an inheritance to all humans who were once orphans in the Earth. We were orphans separated from God because of sin but reunited to Him through the Lamb's bloodline inserted within all who call upon His name. This goes back to having manmade walls between us and God. We are never separated from His love but from His presence. Keep in mind it His presence that allows us to partake in His everlasting love and blessings.

We were all paupers, dirty rags, and heirs to Hell and the father of lies. Let's look at what the Lord God delivered us from, starting with John 8:44, which reads, *"You are of your father the devil, and you want to do the desires of your father. He was a murderer from the beginning and does not stand in the truth because there is no truth in him. Whenever he tells a lie, he speaks from his own nature, because he is a liar and the father of lies."*

Because of one man's sin [Adam], Satan became the father of his entire bloodline. Romans 5:12 confirms, stating, *"Therefore, just as through one man sin entered into the world, and death through sin, and so death spread to all mankind, because all sinned."*

I will stop with Colossians 1:13-17—though I could go on and on—which reads, *"For He rescued us from the domain of darkness, and transferred us to the Kingdom of His beloved Son, in whom we have redemption, the forgiveness of sins. He is the image of the invisible God, the firstborn of all creation: for by Him all things were created, both in the heavens and on Earth, visible and invisible, whether thrones, or dominions, or rulers, or authorities—all things have been created through Him and for Him. He is before all things, and in Him all things hold together."*

YOU were created in God's image for the Son. In the Son, all things hold together. Jesus is Love; therefore, you are held together by Love. You have a Father so in love with you that He wants to lavish His love upon you. He saw you in your blood, rejected by humans who should have adored you yet tossed you aside like a sack of rotten potatoes. He saw you. He sees you still. He remains eternally in love with you, desiring for you to seek and find Him so that He may pour His love upon you and give Himself and His Kingdom to you.

Never let man's rejection define or destroy you. Do not be surprised when earthly mothers, fathers, sisters, brothers, friends, and countrymen abandon, reject, and disappoint you. Be of good cheer—there is One greater and far superior than they! Zechariah 13:6 tells us, *"And someone will say to him, 'What are these wounds between your arms?' Then he will say, 'Those with which I was wounded at the house of my friends.'"*

> "See how great a love the Father has given us, that we would be called children of God; and in fact we are. For this reason, the world does not know us: because it did not know Him...

Do not be surprised, brothers and sisters, if the world hates you…We know love by this, that He laid down His life for us; and we ought to lay down our lives for the brothers and sisters (I John 3:1, 13, 16)."

# Notes

CHAPTER THIRTEEN

*A Forgiving God*

"And when they came to the place called The Skull, there they crucified Him and the criminals, one on the right and the other on the left. But Jesus was saying, 'Father, forgive them; for they do not know what they are doing.' And they cast lots, dividing His garments among themselves (Luke 23:33-34)."

One of the criminals who were hanged there was hurling abuse at Him, saying, "Are You not the Christ? Save Yourself and us!" But the other responded, and rebuking him, said, "Do you not even fear God, since you are under the same sentence of condemnation? And we, indeed, are suffering justly, for we are receiving what we deserve for our crimes; but this man has done nothing wrong." And he was saying, "Jesus, remember me when You come into

Your Kingdom!" And He said to him, "Truly I say to you, today you will be with Me in Paradise (Luke 23:39-43).

Imagine the day Christ went to the cross. He was bloodied, battered, mocked, beaten, wearing a thorny crown, hot, in agony, and walked for miles to His death with blood pouring from His veins, just to be crucified by His own creation for crimes He did not commit. In all this, He was filled with mercy and compassion because He understood the greater good for mankind. He knew He could have easily resisted and rejected the:

1. Cross
2. Humiliation
3. Pain
4. Loss
5. Mercy
6. Forgiveness
7. Kindness
8. Love

He asked the Father if this cup could pass from Him but humbly deferred to the Father's will. One, the thief on the cross Jesus took with Him into Paradise did not go into a profound confession of unforgiveness and forgive his trespassers before Jesus would receive Him unto Himself. No. He accepted [did not deny] Christ for who He was and humbled himself. Two, perfect Jesus forgave those committing treachery against Himself, and asked the Father to forgive them. Three, Jesus understood what was happening on a heavenly, unlimited, eternal level versus an earthly, limited, temporal perspective.

When Jesus said, "*They know not what they do*," He was aware that though they thought they knew what they were doing, spiritually, they had no idea. He saw beyond the surface, which is what Christ's body should do when people come against us. Our Lord did not allow offense to take root, although He could have since He walked in human form. They did not know what they were doing because they had no concept of the spirit realm, Heaven versus Hell, the Kingdom of God versus the kingdom of darkness.

A few years ago, there was a racial issue with a black friend of mine. Whatever the ignorant people did against my friend was bad enough to greatly upset her. When I commented that she should forgive them because "*they knew not what they were doing*," her emotional response was, "*Yes, they did! They knew exactly what they were doing!*" This woman is devoted to the Lord. However, in her offense, she could only process the situation through her feelings [soul].

I had hoped she would see that these oppressors had no concept of what they were doing on a grand spiritual scale. Obviously, they knew they were enacting prejudice, just like the Jews who crucified Jesus. Nevertheless, on an eternal scale, they had no idea. This is where Jesus' supernatural forgiveness comes into play.

We whose spirits are merged as one with Jesus' Spirit [Holy Spirit] should think as He. Throughout the Word, we are told to forgive, not hold grudges, and forgive, forgive, forgive. This is what true love does. Love, God's heavenly, untainted love, is forgiveness personified. This is how I can forgive my first ex-husband without prejudice and anyone else who hurt me along life's highway. Forgiveness is not natural. Forgiveness, then, is supernatural. The adage, "*To err is human, to forgive divine*," is correct.

## Notes

## CHAPTER FOURTEEN

# Freedom for Freedom's Sake

"It was for freedom that Christ set us free; therefore, keep standing firm and do not be subject again to a yoke of slavery (Galatians 5:1)."

"For one who has died has been set free from sin (Romans 6:7)."

"Let no debt remain outstanding, except the continuing debt to love one another, for whoever loves others has fulfilled the law (Romans 13:8)."

"For you were called to freedom, brothers. Only do not use your freedom as an opportunity for the flesh, but through love serve one another (Galatians 5:13)."

Only an eternal, loving God would free wicked mankind—whom He created in perfection from His perfection—who turned on, rejected, and crucified Him for their own evil, sinful ways and deserved slavery and Hell.

The Lord God of Heaven and Earth freed all mankind from condemnation, fear, oppression, lies, betrayal, hatred, malice, ourselves, this perverse generation, and so much more. How much more love could one extend? What more do we expect from God? How has mankind missed this clear extension of God's everlasting love?

We whine, moan, groan, complain, cuss, fuss, belittle, neglect, blame, and mock our loving Creator, yet still expect Him to come through for us. This is shameful behavior at its peak. Regardless, He still forgave us. We must all recognize that mankind, present company included, deserves nothing more than eternal damnation because of our sinful nature. From that stance, His amazing love becomes clearer; hence, easier to recognize and receive.

As discussed in the previous chapter, forgiveness is for our freedom—our unmerited freedom. Unforgiveness binds us to slavery. It is for freedom's sake that Christ set us free. Therefore, when we are unforgiving, we are forsaking God's Kingdom gift of freedom. When I finally forgave my offenders, I became free. The longer we cling to unforgiveness [hatred's equivalent], the longer we are imprisoned within our hearts and minds. Our souls remain wounded. We hurt other people in our woundedness, so we're spreading the very thing we hate. We quench [extinguish, hinder, block] Holy Spirit from being able to move from within us. This is against God per I Thessalonians 5:19.

Additionally, unforgiveness is an act of faithlessness [sin]. Revelation 21:8, Romans 14:23, Romans 3, and more, express the sinfulness of faithlessness. We may have enough faith for fire protection but not enough to live a holy, righteous life through Holy Spirit leading. In knowing to forgive but refuse, we deny and reject God's power to heal us. It often feels better and more powerful to retain unforgiveness than to release it to a higher power—The Holy One of Israel.

I lost count of how many people claim to love the Lord yet deny forgiveness to their offenders. They cite being incapable of such a huge task, the person is unworthy, feeling empty if they release the offender or feelings to God, losing their identity, etc. I have heard all the excuses for not forgiving, all of which fall into the "*faithlessness*" category. It all comes down to where we stand in Jesus. We believe He is sovereign and knows what is best for His creation, or we do not. I am a black-and-white thinking. Either He can empower us to let go, or He cannot—and He can. Either we want to be free, or we do not. Either we desire God's will in our lives, or we do not. We choose to see from a higher plane, or we do not.

Each individual must decide how we want to live, raise our children, teach others, etc. I've had just enough life pains to push me to do things God's way. I have seen how my poor flesh-driven decisions have wreaked havoc on my life, so I deny my flesh as a decision-making participant. Forgiveness is for the forgiver and the recipient.

# Notes

## CHAPTER FIFTEEN

# Story of My Failure and Redemption

> This is My commandment, that you love one another, just as I have loved you. Greater love has no one than this, that a person will lay down his life for his friends. You are My friends if you do what I command you. No longer do I call you slaves, for the slave does not know what his master is doing; but I have called you friends, because all things that I have heard from My Father I have made known to you. You did not choose Me, but I chose you and appointed you that you would go and bear fruit, and that your fruit would remain, so that whatever you ask of the Father in My name He may give to you. This I command you, that you love one another (John 15:12-17).

To recap, I was born-again at age six. I remember it. I meant it then, and I mean it still today more than ever. Regardless of born-again a long time, I only knew basic "*good church*" isms until I returned to Christ from my rebellion.

I knew to read my Bible, be kind, be a Jesus-witness to everyone around me, walk people through the sinner's prayer, and to not drink, smoke, cuss, do drugs, sleep around, etc. In short, I was well-versed in the dos and don'ts of Christianity closely resembling the Bible. I tried my very best to obey. So, what happened to spiral me into seven years of rebellion, you may wonder? In short, I had no clue about dying to self so that Holy Spirit could lead, of which my entire ministry is based.

Once I entered a marriage with an adulterous, philandering, lying, thieving, abusive pedophile, I tried my utmost to make him stop and become the husband I desired. Little did I know how futile my actions were, albeit with good intentions. I was mortified by his actions and did not want anyone— church, family, or friends—to know of his repulsive, repugnant behavior. I did not realize until years later that with my otherwise good intentions, I became a liar, too. I had no clue how to apply God's Word to my situation. And, for full disclosure, I didn't know the Bible well at all, though I thought I did.

Unbeknownst to me, I was a lazy Christian and an even lazier Christ-follower—trust me, there's a distinct difference! Once he left me with a note on the coffee table, bitterness, anger, wrath, malice, deep sorrow, and the blame game burrowed in my heart. My actions became deplorable. Although my sins did not look like my ex-husband's, in God's eye, they were equally sinful, harmful, and detestable. I eventually came face-to-face with that fun fact in due time.

My family and close friends were sure I had lost my mind. No longer did I conduct myself as the *"good church girl."* I gave myself an outward makeover, wearing a naval ring, short skirts, short tops, tanned my skin, cut my hair, and acted emotionally erratic. That was my expression of being lost and heartbroken. I became brutally honest, believing such behavior would undo my ex's perpetual lies. I was always very honest overall, which is why I had been unable to recognize my veiled lie of pretending we had the perfect marriage. I did not set out to deceive; it was an autopilot defense mechanism.

Once I realized I was inadvertently lying by covering his tracks, I vowed to never lie again to anyone about anything, starting with owning up to covering my ex's indiscretions. Again, when I finally repented, I understood brutal honesty is not of God because there is no love. Many other things transpired as I spiraled out of God's control, all chronicled in my autobiography <u>Gauchos, God, and Great Expectations</u>.

Two failed marriages and multiple miscarriages later, I fell on my face before a Holy God in utter surrender. I cried out to Him alone in my bedroom in February 2000. As I mentioned earlier (roughly), *"The church way didn't work. The world's way didn't work. Please, Lord, show me who You are. I have missed something."* After making mess after mess, compounding my problems, I realized I needed a Savior, not just from Hell—I had that, but from myself. And, as Peter said in Acts 2:40, *"…from this perverse generation."*

I was previously 100% saved from eternal Hell. My problem was that I had not matured in Christ enough to live according to God's Word and abstain from being led by my emotions and the world's temptations. I did not know how to surrender all the feelings of blame, bitterness, rage, sorrow, unforgiveness, etc. In that moment of surrender, I experienced God's eternal love for one so wretched as I. I have often stated that I used to love God, then I was infuriated with God, and then I fell head-over-heals in love with God.

The Lord initially took me to Luke 7:47-48 (I recommend reading the entire chapter), where Jesus said, *"For this reason I say to you, her sins, which are many, have been forgiven, for she loved much; but the one who is forgiven little, loves little…your sins have been forgiven."*

As I read those simple words from Jesus, I immediately understood **I have been forgiven much**. When children accept Jesus as their Savior, they haven't sinned much, or at least not big sins, as the world likes to categorize sin. I never regret accepting Christ at six, but I wish someone had taught me early about the sin nature vs. individual sins. Once I began to recognize it was my Adamic nature that Christ died to forgive, it made more sense just how much I needed forgiveness.

Humans tend to play the "*my sins aren't as bad as so-and-so's sins,*" causing them to remain in their "*little sins*" as they see them. This is a deadly game because it keeps many who believe themselves "*of God*" in bondage. I was that person for too long. I needed God's love to cleanse my unrighteous nature and guide me into righteousness—how to walk it [practical application] in everyday life.

What's so beautiful about my redemption is that as I had to endure living in the harvest of sowing sinful seeds, God's grace abounded. Looking back from 2025 to the 1990s, or even the 1980s leading to my painful life choices, I cannot help but see God's lovingkindness all the while. His loving, compassionate hand never left me. He allowed me free will to choose well or poorly. Countless God-signs were ignored, primarily because I didn't understand how Holy Spirit moved, but the Lord was always faithful. He patiently awaited my return and is waiting for your return if you are wayward. He is in love with you just as He is with me.

It was and is in His immovable, indestructible love that I learned how to lean not on my own understanding and to no longer conform to the world's ways, ideologies, and constant temptations. By "*world*," I reference the fleshly temple where I currently dwell, as it is our most fierce temptation and enemy.

# Notes

CHAPTER SIXTEEN

## Nonconformist

> "Do not conform any longer to the pattern of this world but be transformed by the renewing of your mind. Then you will be able to test and approve what God's will is—His good, pleasing and perfect will (Romans 12:2)."

"*Do not conform any longer...*" This indicates we naturally conform to the world but retain the option to cease. We must renew our minds daily to keep ourselves from being underneath the thinking of this condemned world. We ought not let Satan crowd us. Everything seems cloudy when ungodly thoughts are present. We need to have a full view of God's clear will. Take up the Christ-given authority and command the spirit of depression, anxiety, malice, etc., to leave. We do not have to stay under sin's heaviness. Rise above it because we who are in Christ are seated at the right hand of God with Jesus in the heavenlies. This applies to everything not planted in us by God.

Claim what Christ has already said is ours. Get help. We must not allow shame [pride] to keep us from receiving the proper help, ultimately God's love, which is extended through His body of believers. We are one body and should help one another without shame or fear of what others may think. God's Word directs us on how to overcome temptations and emotions because God understands our fleshly nature is prideful and selfish by natural birth. We shouldn't feel ashamed when we sense ungodliness coming but ought to recognize it as an enemy attack. We must gird our loins and team with folks who understand how to help overcome the impulse of self-centeredness [pride, the root of all sin].

Spend time every day praising God for His eternal love poured upon us. We have no time for selfish thoughts when we focus on praising Christ. Praising God regardless of our circumstances confounds the enemy. Satan cannot comprehend it. It is imperative to get our thinking aligned with God's. Seek to know His love's height, width, length, and depth because love covers a multitude of sins. Begin speaking the answer to the problem instead of focusing on the problem.

Stop saying, "*Woe is me*," and begin speaking, "*Praise God. I am healed spiritually, physically, mentally, emotionally, and financially.*" Claim God's promises. Know what He offers and makes available to us through personal accountability and repentance. Put on a garment of praise. I John 5:14-15 states, "...*ask anything in His name, and we will receive the petitions according to His will.*"

God cannot not lie. When we seek a life free of satanic oppression of any kind, Yahweh is faithful to oblige. He wants us free more than we wish freedom for ourselves. He sacrificed His Son to give us freedom before we existed. We must position ourselves to receive His gracious gift. Look how King David handled woefulness:

> [David in the desert of Judah] Because Your love is better than life, my lips will glorify You. I will praise You as long as I live, and in Your name I will lift up my hands. My soul will be satisfied as with the richest of foods; with singing lips my mouth will praise you. On my bed I remember You; I think of You through the watches of the night. Because You are my help, I sing in the shadow of Your wings. My soul clings to You; Your right hand upholds me (Psalm 63:3-8).

Notice David praised God for what he knew in his heart and mind. Our experience and wisdom of God's knowledge save us in troubled times. David was in the middle of a hot, dry, barren desert with no home or wife. Yet, with his lips and heart, he praised his God of salvation and redemption. David did not focus on the problem that would have allowed self-pity to enter his mind and heart. Instead, he focused on God, knowing full well He is faithful, gracious, and a help in times of trouble. At that, he did not stay in the desert. He came out and became a mighty king.

Holy Spirit is our help, aid, comforter, guide, and the internal voice of God Almighty. Without Him, we crumble from brittle, dry bones. With Him, we are pliable, adaptable to any environment, and strengthened in every weakness to be equipped to conquer as one already victorious before the battle begins. Personally, I've learned to not only depend upon Holy Spirit, but I enjoy His constant presence. When we choose to not conform to this world in all its pride [depression, self-loathing, self-absorption, and all things self-centered], Holy Spirit is free to move in and through us. This changes the world instead of the world changing us.

Choose this day whom you will serve: the world and its corrupt order controlled by Satan or the Kingdom of God and its purity through Holy Spirit. Because of God's love, we possess the power of choice.

> Finally, be strong in the Lord and in His mighty power. Put on the full armor of God so that you can take a stand against the devil's

schemes. For our struggle is not against flesh and blood, but against the rulers, against the authorities, against the powers of this dark world and against the spiritual forces of evil in the heavenly realm. Therefore, put on the full armor of God, so that when the day of evil comes, you may be able to stand your ground, and after you have done everything, to stand. Stand firm then, with the belt of truth buckled around your waist, with the breastplate of righteousness in place and with your feet fitted with the readiness that comes from the gospel of peace. In addition to all this, take up the shield of faith, with which you can extinguish all the flaming arrows of the evil one. Take the helmet of salvation and the sword of the Spirit, which is the Word of God. And pray in the Spirit on all occasions with all kinds of prayers and requests. With this in mind, be alert and always keep on praying for all the saints (Ephesians 6:10-18).

"Surely He took up our infirmities and carried our sorrows (Isaiah 53:4)."

The Spirit of the Sovereign Lord is on Me, because the Lord has anointed Me to preach good news to the poor. He has sent Me to bind up the broken hearted, to proclaim freedom for the captives and release from darkness for the prisoners...to comfort all who mourn (Isaiah 61:1-3).

# Notes

## CHAPTER SEVENTEEN

*How to Bask in God's Love*

"If you love Me, you will keep My commandments (John 14:15)."

It is fitting to begin this final chapter with the single verse above. Keeping God's commands is the ultimate unifier between God and man. The biggest issue facing God's people is that most believers don't know the Word as well as they should or believe they already do. As stated earlier, I was that person. I was sure I knew the Word when, in fact, I did not. At least not well enough to keep His commands when it felt like all Hell was breaking loose in my life. I was not as anchored in the Rock of Salvation as I had deceived myself into believing.

Once we know God's Word well, the next step is to obey what we learn. We must be trained to hear His voice and distinguish it from the voice of Satan, demons, and selfish fleshly emotions and opinions.

*"In Him, we have redemption through His blood, the forgiveness of our wrongdoings, according to the riches of His grace,"* is found in Ephesians 1:7. This is excellent information, but we must learn how to live in this redemption instead of just casually speaking, *"I have redemption,"* while living contrary to it.

John 15:4 tells us, *"Remain in Me, and I in you, Just as the branch cannot bear fruit of itself but must remain in the vine, so neither can you unless you remain in Me."* Simply stated, Jesus informs people that staying with or departing from God is entirely in their power. It is a conscious choice we all must make for ourselves. Remaining in Him demands we have no idols above Him. In other words, allow nothing and no one to hold higher value in your life than God, His Word, and His ways. Looking at the Ten Commandments, the first two are:

1. **Command One**: Thou shall have no other gods before Me.
2. **Command Two**: Thou shall not make unto thee any graven image.

I spoke previously of *"the world."* Romans 12:2 states, *"And do not be conformed to this world, but be transformed by the renewing of your mind, so that you may prove what the will of God is, that which is good and acceptable and perfect."*

So, what is the world? It is the world's system ruled by Satan. Also, and this is the part most Christians miss, it is our human shell. There is no more influential "*world*" than the one we inhabit perpetually. It is our world, our fleshly nature from which the Lord redeemed us, yet left us in temporarily. This world of flesh is our greatest adversary. Every day, the fleshly nature longs for everything under the sun set against God. Self is man's greatest idol.

E.g., sexual immorality [anything outside the confines of marriage between a biological male and female (preferably a couple God ordained)], lying, cheating, carousing, drunkenness, breaking covenants [vows], stealing, malice, rage, murder [physical, mental, emotional, spiritual], envy, slander, pride, foolishness, idolatry, sorcery, strife, jealousy, greed, abuse, lovers of self, conceit, fearfulness, faithlessness, etc. (Mark 7:21-23, Galatians 5:19-21, I Corinthians 6:9-10, II Timothy 3:1-5, I Timothy 1:8-11, Revelation 21:8)

Our natural desires are constantly at war against the Spirit of God and His desires. We read in Galatians 5:17, "*For the desire of the flesh is against the Spirit, and the Spirit against the flesh; for these are in opposition to one another, in order to keep you from doing whatever you want.*" The desires of our flesh are always destructive, and our Lord God has made a way to keep us from such destruction.

Seeking first the Kingdom of God will keep us in Christ's love. Matthew 6:33 instructs, *"But seek first the Kingdom of God and His righteousness, and all these things will be provided to you."* Walking in God's love opens to us Heaven's floodgates. We are safe from destruction only when His desires become our desires.

*"Therefore, confess your sins to one another, and pray for one another so that you may be healed. A prayer of a righteous person, when it is brought about, can accomplish much,"* says James 5:16. There is much about this verse worth investigating, but I especially love how confessing our sins to one another keeps us from hiding from God as did Adam in the Garden after he sinned. This instruction is not for our shame but to keep us from shame, guilt, and condemnation.

Matthew 22:37-40 tells us, *"And He said to him, You shall love the Lord your God with all your heart, soul, and mind.' This is the great and foremost commandment. The second is like it, 'You shall love your neighbor as yourself.' Upon these two commandments hang the whole Law and the Prophets."* Luke 10:25-29, a lawyer asked Jesus, *"What shall I do to inherit the Kingdom of God."* Jesus responded, as noted in Matthew, about loving the Lord and neighbors. Then Jesus said, *"Do this and you will live."* Our very life's breath is in loving the Lord above all else and, as an offshoot, love our neighbors as ourselves.

This! Love the Lord, placing no one and nothing above Him. Second, love your neighbor. Many question, *"Who exactly is my neighbor?"* as did the lawyer. Jesus responded by telling him the parable of the good Samaritan. In other words, everyone is our neighbor.

> "I have been crucified in Christ; therefore, it's no longer I who live but Christ who lives in me (Galatians 2:20)."

> "Now those who belong to Christ Jesus crucified the flesh with its passions and desires (Galatians 5:24)."

> "If anyone wants to come after Me, he must deny himself, take up his cross daily, and follow Me (Luke 9:23)."

The above verses instruct us in different words to die to ourselves daily. We cannot live unto ourselves, looking out only for our own interests, if we want to remain in God's love (Philippians 2:4). Ephesians 5:1-2 tells us, *"Therefore, be imitators of God, as beloved children; and walk in love, just as Christ also loved you and gave Himself up for us, an offering and a sacrifice to God as a fragrant aroma."*

Apostle Paul, a sold-out bondservant of our Lord, said in Philippians 2:17, *"But even if I am being poured-out as a drink offering upon the sacrifice and service of your faith, I rejoice and share my joy with you all."* Personally, I long to be a poured-out drink offering unto the Lord. In other words, of my own volition, I empty myself so that others can receive Christ and so the Lord can fill me to the fullest degree with Himself. I belong to Him because He first loved me. He poured Himself out for me, so I choose to do the same for One so selfless.

If it weren't for the love of God, where would I be. Where would you be?

# Notes

# Closing Prayer

Father, thank You for Your patience with me. Help me to learn more and more of the everlasting love You have given condemned mankind. I recognize in utter humility that I, along with the human race, deserve nothing more than Hell. Teach me, most intimately, the height, width, length, and depth of Your eternal love. May I perpetually express Your boundless love to my friends, family, and enemies. Show me how to bless those who curse me as You blessed me while I still cursed You, O Lord. Daily breathe Your holiness into me so that Your love will consume me and move me to righteousness and love. Thank You for allowing me the privilege of experiencing Your love so that wholeness may overtake me. In my wholeness and restoration, I thank You and will always honor You with my every word, thought, and deed, and willingly pour such love upon those still in need of finding Your love. Help me to see as You see, hear as You hear, think with Your mind, love what You love, and hate what You hate. I repent of forsaking Your love and not seeking to better understand the length You

## CLOSING PRAYER

went to save a wretch like me. I praise You for living within me so that I can become an heir to the throne of Heaven. I know I am only dust, yet You lavish Your love on me anyway. Though I fail You, I will maintain a repentant heart to live only as unto You, O gracious Lord of Heaven and Earth! Selah

# Introduction to Christ

If you have come across this book, and you have never been properly introduced to God, this closing is a brief overview of how to come into the Kingdom of God.

## Believe:

> "He then brought them out and asked, 'Sir, what must I do to be saved?' They replied, '*Believe in the Lord Jesus*, and you will be saved (Acts 16:29).'"

> "For John came to you to show you the way of righteousness, and you did not believe him, but the tax collectors and the prostitutes did. And even after you saw this, you did not repent and believe him (Matthew 21:32)."

"*For all have sinned and fall short of the glory of God*" is found in Romans 3:23. You must believe that you dwell in a sinful nature derived from Adam and The Fall of mankind. Secondly, you must believe that Jesus is Lord, that He gave His life for sinful mankind [you], and accept His supernatural gift. It is simultaneously the easiest and hardest decision of anyone's life.

In response to such a belief in the Savior, you can take hold of this Scripture, "*Whosoever shall call on the name of the Lord shall be saved,*" in Acts 2:21." You are "*whosoever.*" Call out to Him—He's waiting.

## Repentance Requirement:

> "This is what is written: The Messiah will suffer and rise from the dead on the third day, and *repentance for the forgiveness of sins* will be preached in His name to all nations…(Luke 24:46-47)."

> "Jesus answered them, 'It is not the healthy who need a doctor, but the sick. I have not come to call the righteous, but *sinners to repentance* (Luke 5:31-32)."

Repentance is a turning and returning. It is turning away [turning your back] from one direction to another, and then turning toward God. It's an act of absolute humility, which is also a requirement for God's presence to rest upon you. Repentance ushers God's grace through humility.

## Baptism to Eternal Life:

> "For *you have died* and your life is hidden with Christ in God (Colossians 3:3)."

"I baptize you with water, but He will *baptize you with the Holy Spirit* (Mark 1:8)."

"He who has believed and has been *baptized shall be saved*; but he who has disbelieved shall be condemned (Mark 16:16)."

"Therefore we have been *buried with Him through baptism into death*, so that as Christ was raised from the dead through the glory of the Father, so we too might walk in newness of life (Romans 6:4)."

"For all of you who were baptized into Christ have clothed yourselves with Christ (Galatians 3:27)."

Baptism takes belief a step further. Baptism, contrary to the modern-day church, *precedes* salvation not *succeeds*. This is not physical baptism, but spiritual. We are to surrender ourselves unto death in the spiritual sense to be able to receive a spiritual new life; hence the Galatians 2:20, "*I have been crucified in Christ; therefore it's no longer I who live but Christ who lives in me.*"

Baptism, metaphorically speaking, is the equivalent of crucifixion, aka death to self. We are "*buried in His death.*" When we come to Christ, we must see ourselves as dead so that we can receive His life. Just praying a *"sinner's prayer"*—which isn't scriptural—is not the same as surrender. Surrender is death.

Think about it like this. When one drowns, it's because they can no longer breathe underwater. If they could, they'd save their own life. When they finally recognize they have no power to rescue themselves, they literally surrender their lives unto a watery death. When we take on Christ's baptism [water of the Word], we must visualize ourselves as *"going under."* We are drowning our natural man because we have no power to save ourselves. In the spirit-realm, we baptize into death all that came from Adam's bloodline. In this death condition, we are now available to take His new life. We are regenerated by a new bloodline from Jesus of Heaven. We take a brand new origin. We are no longer *"of the Earth"* but are *"of Heaven."* This is how we become *"strangers in the land of Earth."*

With this new origin, we must think from the vantage of our homeland, which is the Kingdom of God. This level of surrender causes a person to stop giving in to natural temptations, which brings us back to understanding we have but one nature while occupying space in another nature. You are not your flesh or any of its feelings, desires, or temptations. When tempted with sexual sin [homosexuality, adultery, pornography, pedophilia, or fornication, bestiality], in any form, the flesh wants what it wants, no doubt. However, the surrendered spirit [the real you] within a human shell desires to please the One who gave him a new eternal life. In this condition, he will say "*No*" emphatically because he comprehends that life in the flesh is nothing short of despair, anguish, suffering, and destruction.

Drowning in Christ causes the newness. You cannot have newness without first "*drowning*." Many in the modern-day church preach. "*Accept Christ and then be baptized with water immersion*." However, Scriptures would indicate the opposite. We are to believe in the Father and Son unto salvation, be baptized into His Spirit, then water baptism may follow. The man on the cross received the Kingdom of Heaven through faith, yet was never water baptized. Unfortunately, we often misrepresent the purpose of baptism as if it's merely by water, or a prerequisite to receive God's Kingdom.

## Grace and Repentance:

"Produce fruit in keeping with repentance (Matthew 3:8)."

"Three times I pleaded with the Lord to take it away from me. But He said to me, 'My grace is sufficient for you, for my power is made perfect in weakness.' Therefore I will all the more gladly boast about my weaknesses, so that

Christ's power may rest on me (II Corinthians 12:8-9,)."

"For it is by grace you have been saved, through faith – and this is not from yourselves, it is the gift of God, not by works, so that no one can boast (Ephesians 2:8-9)."

**Definition of Grace:**
1. the free and unmerited favor of God, as manifested in the salvation of sinners and the bestowal of blessings
2. God giving you what you do not deserve (Heaven vs. Hell; life vs. death; peace vs. chaos)
3. the catalyst for an otherwise impossible transformation from the old man of Adam to the new man in Christ

**Definition of Repentance:**
1. to turn from sin and dedicate oneself to the amendment of one's life
2. to feel regret or contrition *leading* to change one's mind
3. to cause to feel regret or contrition
4. to feel sorrow, regret, or contrition

Anyone teaching grace outside repentance and surrender is a false teacher. Surrender and repentance are required to receive God's grace. Yes, we live in the Day of Grace, so it is extended to all mankind on a general level, but in respect to walking in personal grace regularly comes through a heart rent before a Holy God. In this condition of perpetual repentance of the sin-nature, His grace is surely sufficient for you and whatever situational crisis you may face.

When I write "*perpetual repentance*," I mean walking continually in an attitude of cosigning all the lusts of the flesh unto God. It's as the Scripture directs, "*Being ready to punish all disobedience until personal obedience is achieved.*" An attitude of repentance does *not* mean "*self-abase*" because that is sin (Colossians 2:18, 23). Insulting, belittling, and beating oneself is self-abasement—that is not repentance. Repentance insists that you apologize to God for your action(s), go and sin no more, and continue unashamedly going about the Father's business. In true repentance, you are neither ashamed nor boastful in yourself because self is dead to the world and its lusts. Fruit of the Spirit of God can manifest only from a place of humility leading to repentance, which leads to grace.

## Faith:

> "Now faith is confidence in what we hope for and assurance about what we do not see. This is what the ancients were commended for (Hebrews 11:1-2)."

> "Without faith it is impossible to please God (Hebrews 11:6)."

> "Therefore, since we have been justified by faith, we have peace with God through our Lord Jesus Christ, through whom we have gained access by faith into this grace in which we now stand. And we boast in the hope of the glory of God (Romans 5:1-2)."

Faith is an extension of belief, but stronger than belief alone. Even the demons believe and shudder (James 2:19). Faith says, *"I not only believe You exist, but I place all my hope in You,"* unlike the demons. Faith moves the immovable, touches the untouchable, and makes the impossible possible.

## Forgiveness:

> "Therefore, my friends, I want you to know that through Jesus, the forgiveness of sins is proclaimed to you. Through Him, everyone who believes is set free from every sin, a justification you were not able to obtain under the law of Moses (Acts 13:38-39)."

Forgiveness has been extended by God through Jesus to all mankind, whether or not any of us receive it. It was granted to all mankind at the cross and resurrection of Christ. To receive it, all you must do is repent and it's yours. From there, the rest will come with great ease!

Repent to God. Accept His forgiveness. Forgive others. Let go of the shame, guilt, remorse, and condemnation. Let go of the lies, fear, doubt, and anxiety that lead you further and further into darkness.

## A New Master!

> "For sin shall no longer be your master, because you are not under the law, but under grace (Romans 6:14)."

> "If the Son sets you free, you will be free indeed (John 8:36)."

> "But now that you have been *set free from sin* and have become *slaves of God*, the benefit you reap leads to holiness, and the result is eternal life (Romans 6:22)."

> "It is for freedom that Christ has set us free. Stand firm, then, and do not let yourselves be burdened again by a yoke of slavery (Galatians 5:1)."

> "'I have the right to do anything,' you say – but not everything is beneficial. 'I have the right to

do anything' – but I will not be mastered by anything (I Corinthians 6:12)."

"In him and through faith in him we may approach God with freedom and confidence (Ephesians 3:12)."

"You, my brothers and sisters, were called to be free. But do not use your freedom to indulge the flesh; rather, serve one another humbly in love. For the entire law is fulfilled in keeping this one command: 'Love your neighbor as yourself (Galatians 5:13-14).'"

Once you were alienated from God and were enemies in your minds because of your evil behavior. But now He has reconciled you by Christ's physical body through death to present you holy in His sight, without blemish and free from accusation – if you continue in your faith, established and firm, and do not move from the hope held out in the gospel. This is the gospel that you heard and that has been proclaimed to every creature under heaven, and of which I, Paul, have become a servant (Colossians 1:21-23)."

There is no greater gift from God than freedom! There is no greater pleasure or fulfillment in life than serving such a master because this Master is like no other. He is Father, Husband, Comforter, Healer, Redeemer, Forgiver. This is a master I can follow through eternity!

By surrendering to such a magnificent, loving God, you will begin to see that jumping from a ledge to "*end problems*" will no longer appear feasible. Its facade will no longer have the power to overtake you. In Christ, there is no greater place of peace, regardless of the storm, stemming from the liberty found only in knowing and consigning your life to Yahweh. That proverbial ledge will be revealed for what it is—of Satan.

Whatever mess you've concocted, whatever trial besets you, no matter what is happening or for whatever reason, when you submit unto death the nature of the flesh, God commands Himself to take what Satan means against you for evil and turn it for good. I've quoted this Scripture a million times over, yet I will continue to do so because many folks still don't get it. In Christ, there is no dilemma, only benefits from His Kingdom solution. Every horrible, disastrous, despicable situation is a platform God utilizes to catapult His people onto higher ground.

For more detailed information on this matter, I suggest reading the Bible beginning with the gospels to follow the life of Christ, the One who overcame death, grave, and every temptation known to man. He overcame the flesh while living in it. Once He is allowed to take over your life, you too will be able to do as He because His completed work will begin to manifest through you. Additionally, I have written numerous books elaborating on the subjects of knowing your identity in Christ, who you are in the Kingdom of God, how to draw closer to the heart of God, and much more.

If you learn nothing else from this, know that God is in love with you and always will be. He formed you in your mother's womb. He allowed your life to be spared thus far. There is life beyond this crisis. There is joy beyond this sorrow. There is acceptance beyond your rejections. There is gain after your loss. There is life outside death. Be encouraged and of good cheer, for Christ is in love with you today!

# Author's Catalog

1. What was God Thinking?
2-5. Looking for God, 3 volumes or complete series
6-10. Discovering the Person of Holy Spirit, 4 volumes or complete series
11. How to Get it Right: Being Single, Married, Divorced and Everything in Between
12. Thy Kingdom Come: Kingdom vs. Religion
13. Holiness or Heresy: The Modern-Day Church
14. Navigating the Fiery Black Holes of Life: A Book of Faith
15. Talking Yourself off the Ledge: Encouragement at a Glance
16. When All My Strength has Failed
17. Wielding the Sword of the Spirit
18. Learning to Digest the Truth
19. Marriage Beyond Mediocrity
20. Wise as a Serpent, Innocent as a Dove
21. Brotherly Love: A Kingdom Call
22. Casting
23. Extinguishing the Inferno of Anger
24. Wrecked by My Ex: Life Beyond Divorce

25. The War: the Flesh vs. the Spirit
26. Understanding Kingdom Prayer
27. Out of Obscurity
28. Gauchos, God, and Great Expectations
29. Holy Spirit Baptism for Baptists: And Anyone Else
30. A Nation's Achilles Heel: the Perils of Sexual Immorality
31. Living Beyond Life's Residue
32. The Beauty of Discipline: A Book for Parents
33. How Do I Forgive? Letting God Do What We Cannot
34. No Uh-Ohs in Jesus
35. Beyond Grief
36. Just As I Am
37. The Rock
38. Holy Spirit's Presence
39. Suffering: What's Its Purpose?
40. Got Questions? vol 1
41. Praise!
42. The Day of Offense
43. Choices
44. Got Questions? vol 2
45. Not the Lesser Third
46. What is the Lord's Joy? Accessing Joy Amid Hardships
47. If It Weren't for the Love of God

# Author Bio

Alexys V. Wolf is a wife and mother first and is in love with our most Holy God. She earnestly desires to assist people from every walk of life to come out of the darkness of religiosity and into the light of the Kingdom of God. Alexys began her ministry in early 2000, preaching in prisons. She has been a guest on TV, radio, and at conferences, as well as ministering to people globally. She founded the 501c3 ministry, *The Fiery Sword Global Ministries,* in 2007. In 2019, she founded *The Fiery Sword Publications* under *TFSGM*. In 2020, she started a radio show on WDRBmedia called *Better Together: Two Girls and a Bible* with her ministry partner Sandy Renner. A year later, *BTTGAAB* shifted to YouTube. She has authored nearly fifty books and has published many authors. Her mission statement is that of Jesus' found in Luke 4:18-19: "*to preach the gospel to the poor, to proclaim release to the captives, and recovery of sight to the blind, to set free those who are oppressed, and to proclaim the favorable year of the Lord.*"

The Fiery Sword Global Ministries
The Fiery Sword Publications
Lexington, SC 29073

www.thefierysword.com
thefierysword@windstream.net

Made in the USA
Columbia, SC
24 April 2025